Home Ice

Confessions of a Blackhawks Fan

KEVIN CUNNINGHAM

Home Ice

UNIVERSITY OF IOWA PRESS, Iowa City

University of Iowa Press, Iowa City 52242

Copyright © 2017 by the University of Iowa Press

www.uipress.uiowa.edu

Printed in the United States of America

Text design by Richard Hendel

The University of Iowa Press is a member of Green Press
Initiative and is committed to preserving natural resources.

Printed on acid-free paper

ISBN: 978-1-60938-478-4 (pbk)
ISBN: 978-1-60938-479-1 (ebk)

Library of Congress Cataloging-in-Publication Data
is on file at the Library of Congress.

To Eliana

ACKNOWLEDGMENTS

I am grateful to the following people for support, companionship, advice, and shelter: Mark Heineke, who sparked the idea for the book, and Kelly Heineke, for all her patience in Los Angeles; Linda Packer and Stuart Rathje—irreplaceable; Miragh Bitove at the D. K. (Doc) Seaman Hockey Resource Centre in Toronto; the Hockey Hall of Fame; John Pearson; Tony Labriola; Liz Carvlin; Heidi Kolk; Mark Weinberg; Erin Leamas; and Elizabeth Hart. I would also like to thank Jim McCoy, Catherine Cocks, and the entire staff at the University of Iowa Press for their work on behalf of this book.

Home Ice

SKATE-AROUND

1

It was a bright morning. It could be nothing else. Tea had not made me less hoarse by the time I sat down with my breakfast of champions. I can't remember the meal. Leftover Chinese, maybe. I relaxed with it. There was no need to rush online for the game wrap-ups and praise. I had stayed up into the wee hours to see the first stories as they posted.

"How do you feel?" my wife asked.

"I'm glad I lived to see it," I said.

Throughout the 2010 playoffs, each Blackhawks win raised the stakes. The chips piling up on the table represented the accrued emotion of decades past. That emotion would fuel a massive letdown if the Hawks lost. But their success also forced me to risk their very position in my life. Adulthood had granted me a certain perspective on Blackhawks hockey. I learned one of the worst lessons a male sports fan can learn: that whatever happens, life goes on. I point out *male* because I, like millions of other Y chromosomes, rely on sports to provide the sole venue in life where it is acceptable to release emotion. If the Hawks lost, and I gave up on them after forty-some years, how would I fill that void?

Responsibility, worry, and the glacial development of common sense had already caused me to lose touch with the pursuit of rock music, beer, premarital sex, and every other reason to stay alive. But it surprised me to feel hockey slipping away. Hockey and I went back a lot longer than music or beer or even an awareness of sex. Yet there was no denying. No longer did I watch the middle-of-the-night encore broadcasts. Whole games passed without me screaming, though I did grunt a lot. The collars of my jerseys had yellowed because the glorious Indian Heads remained on hangers, unworn and unseen, for years.

Nor did I attend games. Of course, Hawks management had played a part in that by declaring war on its own fan base for the better part of the aughts. But Hawks management had been objectionable since the team's founding.

I wasn't sure what had happened. Once, my relationship with the Hawks had been passionate, if always conducted in an atmosphere of impending disappointment. Now, though, my Hawk fandom felt like a tired relationship, where islands of volcanic emotion occasionally arose from a sea of polite disinterest formed by long habit.

The Blackhawks may have hit rock bottom circa 2004, but they had last contended—I mean, truly had a shot that did not involve an imponderable chain of fluke occurrences—just ten years earlier. A decade is a long time in sports, but it's not a black hole. The team's dissolution, a series of events that included the massive level of self-deception necessary to see a blockhead like Tyler Arnason as a star, clinched but did not spark my drift away from Hawks obsession.

Adulthood played a part, of course. Its demands already made it hard to carve out time for the *Hockey News*, and you can read that thing in about eight minutes. Now my wife was pregnant. Even as I ate the celebratory breakfast, she sent our then-fetal daughter oatmeal and fruit. How angry would I be when I wasted three hours of my precious free time to watch a tilt with the Predators that ended in a shootout loss?

Philadelphia putting some hurt on the Hawks early on allowed me to ponder a heretical silver lining to a Hawks Stanley Cup loss. If it happened, God forbid, I'd have the excuse I needed to relegate the Blackhawks to the passing interest category. The hours of my life thus regained could go toward refining nanotechnology or attending my daughter's ballet recitals.

Or, I thought, maybe a period of self-imposed exile would allow me to have it both ways. I'd be a boffo father free to attend all the events of a busy twenty-first-century childhood. Then, by the time the Hawks made a run at the 2028 Cup (right on schedule), my daughter would have headed off to freshman orientation at the Sorbonne. I would have all the free time I needed to watch what by then would be a fourteen-round postseason.

But . . . the Blackhawks had won. In 2010, before the era of ape conquest, they had won.

"Were they drinking champagne from the Cup?" my wife asked, probably not intending an uppercase *C* in *cup*.

"The French-Canadians, maybe," I said. "Hockey players seem to mostly like beer."

Like most Hawks fans that day, I was experiencing a kind of happiness immune to cynicism. But I knew that my joy, while genuine, was a small thing compared to the bender I would have embarked upon had the Hawks won in, say, 1995. Yes, I had changed. Yada yada.

But why did I care about a hockey team, this hockey team, in the first place? And why was I so sad I had navigated the change in my feelings toward it?

● It is traditional in a sports book to claim that the team under examination inspires a unique form of suffering. Admittedly, handing Chris Chelios to Detroit caused me to break out in a rash that lasted for twelve years. But followers of most National Hockey League teams, of most sports teams, can provide a timeline hash-marked with lamentations, disappointment, and dermatological problems. While the Hawks have provided their fans with many painful moments, the most that can be said by way of superlatives is that the franchise shares a legacy of breathtaking stupidity and venality with—well, okay, just an elite few.

Let's try again. True, the Hawks' team executives spent 1997 to 2005 running around in circles while the *Benny Hill* theme music played in the background. Spare a thought, though, for the sufferings of a contemporary Oilers fan, one too young to remember the 1980s. Sure, the Hawks dealt away Phil Esposito for no discernible reason. They ran off Bobby Hull in a hail of insults and traded Jeremy Roenick at his peak due to some weird sense of violated *omerta*. But they didn't sell off the greatest player of all time (at age twenty-seven), or see their sleazy owner almost destroy the team, or fall into a whirlpool of mediocrity (albeit after winning a title without Gretzky) that lasted thirty years, or watch the league's financial structure change in ways that made it impossible for them to compete.

Whatever the pains, Patrick Kane's epic goal and all that led up to it saved my fading ardor for our heroes and for NHL hockey in general. Damn the dulling effects of adulthood. I suddenly had motivation to learn about the salary cap, to revive my terrible Pat Foley impression, to put the jerseys in the wash.

Again the question: why had a Hawks championship meant so much to me? To all of us? God knows I played no part in the triumphant march, had shed no blood or cash. Sometimes I *felt* as if I had a bleeding ulcer, but a real one had burned a hole in Joel Quenneville's stomach. As time passed I wondered more and more about where this love of hockey, and in particular the connection with the Blackhawks, had come from.

● I never played ice hockey. Though I'm reasonably athletic, preschoolers can outskate me. The pack animals in donkey hockey charity games can outskate me.

Nor did I live in any sort of hockey hotbed as a kid. In fact, for long periods of my life I followed the game through print or the highlights tacked on to the end of sportscasts on very slow news nights.

This separation from the game wasn't my fault. My parents refused to move to Toronto. Furthermore, when I was a kid, Evel Knievel got more airtime than the NHL. Even after the Miracle on Ice allegedly introduced hockey to a mass audience, American cable channels preferred Australian rules football to the NHL. The situation changed a little when the USA Network and then ESPN adopted the league for a time. But the Blackhawks, languishing in their post-1973 doldrums, seldom if ever attracted the attention of the embryonic cable titans.

As for the inheritance theory—sports loyalties passed from fathers to sons and daughters—it is true my dad introduced me to the Blackhawks. A native Kentuckian, he moved to Chicagoland in his teens and followed Chicago sports with the avidity of any late convert, if also with the fatalism of a native.

The thing is, Dad was not a big hockey fan. Sure, he checked in if the Hawks were on, once the NHL returned to TV. He wished them well. He kept up with what was going on enough to hold a conversation. As is the case with most of Chicago, though, the Bears were his main team. Thus, according to inheritance theory, I should spend Sundays—and some Thursdays, Saturdays, and Mondays—racked out in a metaphorical recliner drinking a metaphorical six of Bud Light with the rest of Real America. Yet I haven't watched pro football on a regular basis in years.

Studying my impending parenthood and what it might turn into down the road, I thought it important to understand the source of my obsessions, in order to better support those of my daughter. As a parent I hoped to avoid the unnecessary friction I had with my folks. God knows, there will be enough necessary friction over the car, the chastity belt, etc. It's easy for distance to develop between loved ones. I wanted to avoid handing down past mistakes to the next generation.

Many of my passions manifested at an early age. Except for a love of music, all seem to have sprung up without any connection to the interests of loved ones, influential peers, or mentors. All of my obsessions baffled my parents, even frustrated them. Dad wondered about why I'd learn to type when I could replace a distributor cap. And so on.

In calmer moments I dismissed my own concern as just another of the irrational worries that afflict new parents. The question of how the Blackhawks entered my life continued to knock around my brain and led to other questions. It took time to access the memories that led me to the inadequate answers. Thanks to the Cup win, I could for once put aside angst and see the *pleasures* offered by the Hawks, pleasures unique to them in some cases, and general to hockey in others. This newfound if short-lived clarity didn't explain how I'd come to love the team. But it clued me in to how someone could, and that was a start.

THE MAGAZINES

2

I read four books in third grade. Though memory is unreliable, I am confident of the figure because anything that unimpressive is probably true.

The first was *Stuart Little*, a kids' book about a mouse. The second was *Chariots of the Gods*—only the classics for me—and the third an astronomy book by Patrick Moore, one of those fantastically crusty British crackpots who wore a monocle and after decades of bachelorhood declared women had ruined the world. What can I say? Some little boys dig on dinosaurs. For me it was outer space. Learning about the Messier catalog, which numbers certain objects like galaxies and nebulae, prepared me for French-Canadian hockey names.

I stand behind my last choice: Stan Mikita's *I Play to Win*. As the rest of the reading list shows, I had until that time never read a chapter book by a sane person.

No offense to Stan, but I doubt I made it through the entire book. That was just my attention span then.

A life story about matters off and on the ice, *I Play to Win* remains worth reading even now, though Mikita's recent *Forever a Blackhawk* covers and elaborates on some of the same material. *I Play to Win* came out in 1969, when Mikita—

with two Hart Trophies and four Ross Trophies on his resume—
was one of *the* stars in the NHL. Once a penalty-prone pest nick-
named *Le Petit Diable*, Mikita had reformed to become a Lady
Byng winner by the time he turned to writing.

There's no false modesty in the book. Mikita's proud of his ac-
complishments, and rightly so. What's endearing is that he puts
his story out there in an unaffected way. He can write that he
thought he deserved a number-two center spot on an All-Star
team over Jean Béliveau, but it doesn't sound petty; it doesn't
even sound as if he thought twice about it.

His reflections on his selection as Most Valuable Player:

> This is the Oscar of hockey. It means that people consider
> you the best player in the league out of more than two
> hundred—*whether you are or not*—and there can't be higher
> praise.

I learned all of that rereading *I Play to Win* as an adult, though.
I recalled only two parts from my third-grade study.

First, the magazines. Mikita shows up for his first youth-
league practice in second-hand skates and with magazines tied
around his legs for pads. I never forgot that detail. I once used it
in one of my many half-finished novels. For years I thought the
magazines illustrated Stan's childhood poverty. As it turns out,
he didn't grow up poor. Joe Mikita (the uncle who brought Stan
to Canada from Czechoslovakia, and who Stan called Dad) built
houses, and the family did okay. Either Stan didn't ask for pads,
or Joe Mikita wisely waited to see if the kid was serious about
hockey before making the investment.

Then there's the story of how Stan came to Canada. I found it
harrowing, as a nine-year-old, that a kid around my age left behind his family to move thousands of miles away, to a country

where he didn't know the language, where he had to change his name and trade a familiar farm life he liked for St. Catherines, Ontario.

At first Stan considered it an adventure. After all, the trip began with a train ride. Then in Prague, about to leave for France and the ship to cross the Atlantic, he realized his parents would remain behind and broke down. I understood that emotion. I found it moving when I reread the book a few months ago. That he continued to think for years about going back is heartbreaking, though obviously things worked out.

In St. Catherines he learned hockey terms as some of his first English words. Kids also taunted him by calling him a DP, or displaced person. Children can be monsters, obviously, but picking on someone because you think (wrongly, yet) that he's a war refugee? The guy doesn't have enough problems coming from a country that split the 1940s between the Third Reich and the Red Army? What's wrong with being a DP, anyway? Why would non-DPs be so down on it? Did Canadian parents tut-tut about how escapees from a communist takeover would lower property values?

No doubt some kids threw down the name just to rile up Stan, in the way kids have of hurting others for no reason other than joy. Yet Mikita dealt with it as an adult, too. DP was a favorite insult of Mikita's nemesis, the Montreal Canadiens star Henri Richard:

Richard and I always have had a touchy relationship. We've even had a fight or two or more. I treasure one of those with him, because it's one of the few I've ever won. . . . What usually touched off our scraps was a stick or elbow in the right place. Henri would call me "DP" and I'd snap back with "Frog" or "Pea Soup"—because he's French Canadian.

Pea soup! If that's considered a slur, I apologize for laughing. Let's repurpose it to tease kids possessed by the Devil.

We both wound up in the penalty box one game after a fight. Then I guess Henri glared at me and I looked at him and I kind of snickered. He said, "Say, what you laugh at? You a DP. You come to dees country. You even don' speak so pretty good da Engleesh." That heavy, broken accent sounded as funny as hell under the circumstances.

Based on my reading habits of the time, I suspect I put down *I Play to Win* when I realized Stan wasn't going to get abducted by aliens. I don't remember reading about Mikita's early career, but I'm guessing I made it that far, because I was always on the lookout for a moneymaking deal—those wax worms with the colored syrup inside didn't buy themselves. Possibly, I picked up the book in the first place to cadge insider knowledge on becoming a pro hockey player and making a ton of money. The impulse, while built on the myth that 1970s hockey players got rich, did speak to an actual truth. My family needed the money.

By the time he reached juniors, it seemed to me that Mikita had it all. First, he went through a teen greaser phase. Fonzie on skates. Awesome. Even better, he made $60 a week, plus $15 under the table. Big money, clearly, and this was before he beat Hawks GM Tommy Ivan out of an extra five grand on his signing bonus. Mikita even quit school to turn pro. It was like a dream.

THE MUNRO DOCTRINE

3

It sounds too perfect, but it's possible I owned the coveted Bobby Hull table hockey extravaganza with the puck-dropping gondola-slash-scoreboard over center ice. I can't swear to it. Mom loved a bargain. It wouldn't surprise if that at Christmas she scored some knockoff Hungarian game at a garage sale. But I don't think so. My game's player pieces were plastic, for one thing, and Iron Curtain countries made toys out of cement. Also, Mom worked the Sears catalog hard, and Sears sold the Hull model made by Munro.

Table hockey gave me a tool for working out the game's finer points. Admittedly, though, it best lent itself to fantasy via an imperfect re-creation of actual play. None of the slots allowed for a rush the length of the rink, for instance, and there wasn't enough space for a majestic cross-ice pass. Nor was offsides a concern—a good thing, since I hadn't seen the Peter Puck episode explaining it when my parents gave me the game.

So it took imagination to relive what you saw on TV. That applied to the players as well as the action. Not because the players were pieces of plastic. I can think of a half-dozen NHLers today who are as stiff and ungifted as a table hockey forward. I'm sure that many suited up then, too. And not because every sticker was of a serious-looking white man. That reflected the real game, too, though it seemed odd that the same six guys played for everyone, and that none of them looked like Stan Mikita.

The uniforms, though. Recognizable team colors, similar detailing on the sleeves and socks—but Munro either had not licensed the official NHL logos or had bid lower than Coleco, their main competitor, or had found the geniuses then running NHL teams unwilling to sell. Whatever the case, a player just wore a city name—a state name for the Seals and North Stars—across the chest. It was like replacing Warhol's portrait of Wayne Gretzky with a bumper sticker that said "Painting."

My excitement over owning the game far outweighed the aesthetic lapses, however. Anyway, I couldn't complain. I did my part, too. Like a million other kids, I scribbled player names on the back of the uniforms. We kids were ahead of our time, by the way. It took until the mid-seventies for NHL teams to put names on sweaters, and then they did it just for nationally televised games.

The French names led to mistakes. There are a lot of ways to misspell J. P. Bordeleau, and even more when you think his first name is Japey. I also refused to let sad reality get in my way. Bobby Hull remained a Blackhawk, the World Hockey Association be damned.

When no one else was around to play a game, I set the Montreal players in various positions and practiced trying to pass around them. I soon learned to propel the puck with the base of the player as well as the stick—the table hockey equivalent to kicking it in—and found out you could shoot the puck off the side of the goalie to score, assuming the goalie was just kind of sitting there because no one held its rudder.

But living out in the country often left me wanting for an

actual game. My oldest sister had no table hockey mojo. My then-youngest, now-middle sister was one year old and kept trying to eat the puck.

Friends and cousins, thank God, made the scene on weekends. The house then filled with a din made up of spinning rods, too-hard slamming of players up and down the slots, the clack of the puck, the hollow sound of it rolling across the wooden floor when it flew out of the rink, nonstop screaming, choking noises from my one-year-old sister, and the occasional, always accidental goal-related swearing. I added to the noise by pronouncing Yvan Cournoyer's last name as Cournoyerererererer. Letting it fade to echo, you dig. I cannot express how funny this was to me and only to me. I repeated it until my friends wanted to leave. Then I'd keep doing it until I had no friends.

Owning the table hockey game gave me 24/7 access for practice. I figured I'd become a table hockey ace in a few weeks, tops.

Yet despite the advantage, I was the California Golden Seals of the Midwest. My career record—I'm estimating here—was 0-847-2. I took the two ties off my grandmother. She fell asleep both times.

Fate has chosen to make me bad at the games where I try hardest. I spent my childhood trying to beat my mom at gin rummy. Then I worked with words my entire adult life only to lose at Scrabble whenever I play: lose to drunks, to dyslexics and recent immigrants, to children who convince me *ziqax* is a word, to people simultaneously playing and pilling their cats—anybody. I just don't have good game instincts, as Bill Clement might say. Seriously, I've lost at Ouija.

There was one time I almost broke the table hockey streak, though. Terry and Jerry (my twin cousins) and I set up a play-off system. The Boys, as everyone from family to the local police called them, were two years older than me. That matters in childhood, but it also offered me a chance at victory over a superior foe. Not that redemption would be easy. The Boys had it all over me when it came to NHL-level aggressiveness. In the ecosystem of childhood, they were wolverines, and I was a tree sloth that had just become a Quaker. Granny, a product of pre-PC times, often called them wild Indians. For years they shrugged off fantastic injuries, took every dare, defied common sense and actuarial tables, and watched out for me.

I almost beat Jerry. Once. I only have his promise—and his real effort during the game—as evidence he was not taking it easy on me. At one point I led by three goals. That isn't an insurmountable deficit in table hockey. But time had run short by the time Jaype Bordello finished his hat trick.

As I stood there at the end of our dining room table, I imagined what it felt like to win. I should have been concentrating on the goalie rutter.

Jerry ripped off a goal to cut the lead to two. Time remained on my side, but I had no concept of running down the clock. I was eight—I barely understood time at all. My nerve crumbled. Then the next goal released a rushing river of frustration. I was blind with it. Goal followed goal. Jerry won going away.

By chance, I'm writing this anecdote about twenty-four hours after the Hawks took a 2-0 lead into the early second period at Edmonton and lost 8-4. Silver lining of that collapse: I now feel better about my playoff loss forty years ago. I think I'll even let go of seeing myself as table hockey's Charlie Brown. I can almost hear a chorus of current Hawks defensemen saying, "Five cents, please."

The table hockey game, like a lot of my toys, did not enjoy a long life. A misplaced foot or elbow (the details are vague; it remains a cold case in family lore) opened a fault line down one side of the Blackhawks' offensive zone. The cheap particle board resisted repair by glue, and the puck wouldn't have ever slid true again. We moved after I finished third grade. As far as I can remember, the game didn't make the trip.

COMPETING FAITHS

4

When not playing on the table, I watched real hockey with Willie Bea, my grandmother. I had no choice. No one else I knew cared about hockey.

Willie Bea didn't need to watch television. She was an active sixtysomething. Not an unspent overachiever running marathons, mind you, but a five-tool domestic player (clothes, dishes, cooking, sewing, cleaning). I believe hockey represented a safe alternative to one of the outdoorsy activities a grandchild might prefer. After all, the broadcasts began in mid-winter, and, in those days, when sixty was the old sixty and orthopedics had not yet advanced enough to save Bobby Orr's knees, slipping on the ice had enormous consequences. Better to stay inside.

Willie Bea watched sports all the way into her eighties. Her tastes ranged far beyond the *NHL on NBC*. The Harlem Globetrotters, tape delays of Frazier or Ali or Foreman licking some challenger, whatever the Norwegians were doing with skis that week on *Wide World of Sports*—if she had switched the laundry and no one had thrown up, she was there until she dozed off.

To be honest, I think even she considered hockey second-tier. Pro basketball was very much her game. I say that because hoops kept her excited enough to stay awake. At times she raised her shrill granny voice—in a tone that reminded everyone of the *Beverly Hillbillies* namesake, or a ptero-dactyl—to tell someone to "get it, get it" or "ruuuuun." Once a game she would see Moses Malone or the like and say in awed tones, "Now *that's* a big man." Someone told me a possibly apoc-ryphal story that Willie Bea had played basketball as a girl. Since some girls' leagues played a nine-on-nine game in the twenties, I imagine you could roster a string-bean four-elevener and be okay.

But pro hoops were about as hard to find on TV as hockey, and, anyway, she wasn't that discriminating.

The *NHL on NBC* picked up the hockey season around the first of the year. Willie Bea and I watched these midseason games in black and white. *Black and white* was a primitive form of visual communication that allowed a viewer to see *Laverne & Shirley* as a dog did. I had no problem with it. I didn't even notice. You went to my grandmother's place, you watched the B&W; it was as nor-mal as her rotary phone with the ear-splitting ringer or the fact she could remove her teeth, uppers and lowers. You didn't need color for hockey, anyway, thanks to the big logos on the sweaters.

In my memory the *NHL on NBC* always broadcast a game that featured two of the Flyers, Bruins, or Canadiens. It also seemed like there was a bench-clearing brawl once per contest. Neither is the truth, though neither is far from it, either. NBC also showed Detroit five times during the first season, more than any other team. The Hawks were always good for two or three games per year. Buffalo and Atlanta, however, played only a few of these marquee games during the *NHL on NBC*'s three-year run, and California's sole appearance was at Chicago in early 1975 (Hawks win).

I liked watching games with Willie Bea because she had no problem with my questions. Granted, my dad answered what-ever nonsense I came up with, but my ignorance detracted from his immersion in the game in front of him. Willie Bea's flaw as a mentor was that she knew nothing about ice hockey. She had spent most of her life in western Kentucky. Ice there is something that goes into your glass of breakfast Coke. Unfortunately, I had yet to master the game's nuances by the time the *NHL on NBC* made the scene. Even more unfortunately, I couldn't take a hint.

ME: Why do they stop playing sometimes when the puck goes all the way down to the other end, but not all the time?

HER: Mmmm.

[Pause]

ME: See? That guy shot it a long way but then they kept playing.

HER: Look at them go.

[Five minutes later]

ME: Now they shot it the other way and stopped.

HER: [click of displeasure] That mean boy is fighting again.

Peter Puck, the animated sage of millions, the *Schoolhouse Rock* of the rink, set me straight on icing. I liked P2 and, thanks to YouTube, I still do; in fact I dream of founding a charter school where Peter Puck videos play every morning at 10:15. Past bad habits had socialized me to enjoy his lessons, too, since the clips featured the same god-awful animation and incongruous, poorly looped sound effects I laughed at every Saturday morning on *The Amazing Chan and the Chan Clan*.

Toward the end of the *NHL on NBC* era, we moved to an actual town. The good news: my grandmother lived in the town, so I saw her and hockey more often. The bad news: my mother decided we had to become Catholics.

The woman led us through a spiritual buffet. I couldn't even keep all the faiths straight. One put up a Christmas play where my friend Paul Grenier began shooting at Baby Jesus with his shepherd's crook. Another one didn't even declare a denomination. It did declare PREPARE YOURSELF TO DIE on the big sign out front.

Catholicism was a return to home ground for Mom. She came from minor Roman royalty. One of her uncles or great-uncles, Father Charles Dismas Clark, was famous enough to be the subject of the 1961 film *The Hoodlum Priest*.

Mom must've figured she had to go back to bedrock to save our souls. Always ahead of her time, she outsourced and, despite being the sole real Catholic in the family, made my devotedly irreligious father take us to Mass. Not only did churchgoing deprive him of sleep, it forced him to miss the first fifteen minutes of the *NFL Today*. It takes a real father to sacrifice Jayne Kennedy in favor of a groovy guitar mass, all just to keep his heathenish kids right with the sisters and, less importantly, Jesus. The *NHL on NBC*, fortunately, started at 3 p.m.

A small-town Catholic school is a tight community. To some degree the community lives inside a citadel to avoid the rednecks and Methodists and other local unfortunates headed for the lake of fire. I started spending Sunday afternoons playing with other larval papists. Having neighbors again also gave me the chance to horse around with new friends.

These friends, like the rest of America, had no interest in hockey. Low ratings soon sent the *NHL on NBC* into a thirty-one-year hiatus after the Hawks and North Stars closed out the 1975 regular season.

It's no coincidence I took the Blackhawks more fully into my identity around the same time Mom shoved me into the deep end of Roman Catholicism. These two lifestyle choices shared a cultish insularity. Both also involved rules that, to a newcomer, made no sense whatsoever.

But the parallels went further. Hockey and Catholicism both featured people with funny names (Guy, Ignatius), both revolved to some degree around bread products (biscuit, wafer), and both—to make the obvious joke—offered opportunities for prayer. Every fourth Saturday or so, I sat in a sin bin where a guy in a black-and-white uniform always gave me a minor penalty. (An easy-going kid, I contended for the Lady Byng when it came to mortal sins.)

The eighty-game hockey season also equaled the Vatican's season schedule: the Sabbaths (fifty-two), Wednesdays during the school year (about thirty), first Fridays of the month during the school year (eight or nine), and non-Sunday big-time holy days (four or so). I lasted longer as a practicing Catholic than the NHL did as a source of network programming. But only a little longer. Another baby arrived two years after I started at St. James. After that, my parents no longer had the energy for church. I wasn't going to beg to go.

I retired from active duty in the One True Faith just as I less willingly parted from hockey. NBC, tired of low ratings, booted the NHL from its programming calendar and left a great sport to mere pockets of fans in selected northern cities and to electronics enthusiasts with enough imagination to tap into the feeds of Canadian TV satellites.

Whatever games I watched that last season I saw while visiting Willie Bea. I can only guess at which ones. January weather no doubt kept me indoors for the aforementioned Seals-Hawks contest. I don't remember the game, but it sounds like riveting TV. "Glad I didn't have to do color for that one," Mikita told the papers. "Chicago just puts you to sleep," added the Seals' Len Frig.

Maybe I watched Boston thump the Hawks in early March. But for sure I tuned in for the two televised Flyers-Bruins tilts, may have even seen the famous Terry O'Reilly–Dave Schultz fisticuffs, round umpteenth, in mid-February.

I'm sure I missed the Hawks and North Stars on April 6, though. A historic game, it turned out, but at the time I had no idea free TV would become a no-go zone for the NHL—outside of a single Finals game broadcast—until the 1990s. Even if I'd known the game's import, there's no way Mom and Dad were letting me stay inside once the weather turned mild. They had just spent six months cooped up with a bunch of kids. To go through a few more hours of that? With the TV on? And me shouting?

None of the other networks stepped in for NBC. Better to fill time with ratings gold like rodeo. For a long time I would ask Dad to switch around the channels on Sunday afternoons during the commercial breaks of football games. Would we find hockey again? I wondered, hoped, prayed. Nope. Just a guy named Randy being gored.

BIRTH OF THE UNCOOL

5

The child psychologist I should've seen would never have considered me a carefree personality. Burdened with a firstborn's seriousness—a trait amplified by the guilt multiplier of exposure to a gentle guitar-mass Catholicism that put solving the problems of Ecuadoran peasants on fourth graders—I never learned to give myself over to the joyful extremes of emotion that ought to be a part of healthy sports fandom. My friends of the era had an enviable ability to rave about the triumphs of "their" Cowboys or Crimson Tide, could parade with forefingers held aloft and lean on their parents' car horns until pelted with neighbors' shoes. I already suffered the agony of victory. To this day a Hawks playoff win makes me put my head down and moan, "Thank God." Making the expectation of disappointment central to my fan experience taught me to forego joy in favor of the inferior catharsis produced by relief.

Not that it mattered. I didn't see the Blackhawks enough to be scarred by them, of course, but in any case the only losses that brought me to extremes of feeling in childhood involved a team I actually played on losing by slaughter rule while I struck out six times. Not until young adulthood did I begin to react to final scores with anger, tears, and all the other saliva-producing emotions.

● Some of my enthusiasm for the Hawks had roots in a nascent fascination with fringe culture. Ice hockey lacked the outsider cred of, say, listening to a hand-lettered Guided by Voices cassette in 1988, or owning *The Book of the SubGenius*. Exile from television placed hockey, by definition, outside the mainstream. Liking it marked one as just a little bit unorthodox.

I know, I know, what could be more mainstream jock than rooting for oft-violent white boys, however boldly toothless? But inhabiting a universe that barely recognized hockey's existence, I saw it as the subversive sport, more recognizable and comprehensible than Australian rules football, the sport of the era deemed cool (as in extreme) by my peers. Maybe the surgeons and financiers sitting at the glass enjoyed being a little punk rock in their sports fandom, a little transgressive, as we say in the academic publishing business.

When I state the NHL is a cult sport in the United States, I do so facetiously, aware that fans are not subject to mind-control techniques, though hockey figures—from execs to players, even trainers—have a long history of practicing what Robert Jay Lifton calls "milieu control," controlling the flow of information to manipulate others. The average NHL attempt at milieu control comes across as too laughable to be threatening to all but the weakest minds, i.e., "Putting his face into the boards was an accident" or "The owners are losing money."

Anyway, unable to watch games, I kept the fringe flag flying.

I enjoyed permanent residency in the lower regions of the middle class, but I found the money to accumulate boxes of trading cards. Baseball and football cards, of course. Also *Star Wars* cards. Also *Charlie's Angels* cards, a surprising number of which featured Cheryl Ladd in circus costumes. Eager to merge two addictions, I scoured the low-end retailers and convenience stores of the Midwest hoping to add hockey cards to my collection. I never saw a single packet. Not even an empty box. That's where pro hockey existed in the late seventies zeitgeist: kids preferred to collect cardboard of the Bionic Woman.

See? Fringe.

At some point I decided to become a cartoonist/comic-book artist—like the *Star Wars* cards, a station stop en route to geekdom. What's most sad about the detour is I believed success, once achieved, would offer financial help to my family.

Hockey figured in my works. One of my supervillains, name forgotten, resembled a goaltender, an intimidating visual composition reduced to low comedy when I pitted him against a superhero named Plungerman. I sketched hockey scenes from magazine photos, from Archie-Reggie grudge matches, from library books. One of my favorite Christmas presents ever was a paint-by-numbers set of hockey scenes, a gift so thoughtful I actually expressed a civilized level of gratitude to my parents. I spent the entire holiday crouched over a picture and ignoring my relatives, consumed by the chance to work at my talent level for visual art.

The paint-by-numbers kit, like the table hockey game, foreshadowed the way others would identify me with hockey. The sport in essence became an aspect of my personality. For male friends wary of showing emotion and female friends reluctant to show too much interest, for co-workers and classmates and mere acquaintances, to say nothing of the none-of-the-aboves roped into attending one of my birthday parties, hockey served the vital social role of providing others with ideas for gifts.

We all rely on this shorthand. A throwaway comment by my wife, for instance, led to her being given a pile of Curious George memorabilia, first by the sister who heard the comment, and then by the rest of us piggybacking on the idea. Whether it did her any good—beyond feeling cared for, I mean—remains unclear, but in the end the monkey-emblazoned garbage can, lunchbox, and dreidel served us well, as our daughter has taken collectibles with modest prospects for cost appreciation and transformed them into beloved playthings.

Hawks fandom was also a godsend in terms of family peace. My dad and sisters, having lost contact with me on any deeper level, nonetheless expressed their love at the holidays by adding to the rack of Blackhawks-themed clothing in my closet. Friends preferred to give me books. I received *Crunch: A History of Fighting in the NHL* at a Tiny Lounge celebration. A girlfriend once passed along a battered but unbowed *Hockey Heroes of Today*, published by Random House when the hockey heroes included a great many balding Canadians and only some of the goalies wore masks. She also unearthed *Norman Plays Ice Hockey*, the story of a turtle that must play against a team composed of a weasel and other carnivores. Plus their goalie is an elephant.

To say nothing of the Lego hockey players and die-cast Zambonis and hockey-themed sticker books aimed at kindergartners. Time and again, I have thanked the Hawks for allowing me to feel loved while others have thanked the Hawks about not having to think too hard about a gift. Thus is civilization maintained.

THE LIMPING SUPERMAN

6

I know how Washington Bullets fans felt about Michael Jordan, because Bobby-Orr-to-the-Blackhawks brought the same thrill to fans of his new team and the same sense of melancholy to everyone else. Orr stood at the zenith of hockey stardom in the 1970s. In fact, he had achieved such notoriety in the pop culture at large that non-hockey fans recognized his name. Bobby Orr was so famous he could have fought Superman. Had there been a whitesploitation genre, Orr might have retired from hockey to star in *Shaft Goes to Regina.*

He was almost everyone's favorite player, mine included. It sounds disloyal, but, remember, I'd seen the Bruins far more than the Blackhawks. That I remain an avid consumer of Orr media testifies to how strongly we imprint on our heroes as kids. When YouTube matured into a form that gave a searcher a reasonable chance to find whatever dumb idea came to mind during a soon-to-be-unproductive workday, I at first wasted hours watching eighties music videos. But then I hunted for Orr highlights, watched without thinking or analyzing, in a *pure* way, as a child would watch it and had watched it, unencumbered by cynicism or distraction or the idea that a grown man should not have favorite athletes—watched it, in other words, with joy, a feeling so rare in my everyday life that it left me momentarily confused.

It would be easy to dismiss the "Orr evening"—"Orr week"—as an in-the-moment thing. But it happened again. Same emotion, same admiration, same happiness. My wife and I both loved Vancouver and absorbed the 2010 Winter Olympics opening ceremony. From past experience I knew the festivities would feature Canadian heroes of one kind or another. There was Anne Murray, the empress of easy listening, rightly presented as an iconic personification of the host nation.

"Hey," I exclaimed, interrupting my own off-key verse of "Snowbird."

"What?" my wife said, startled.

"That's Bobby Orr. Holy crap. Bobby Orr."

It made the evening for me. I don't fully understand why. No making fun of his white suit, no notice of the other flag bearers, just watching Bobby Orr with a slack jaw and tears in my eyes.

● Reports had the Hawks shelling out $3 million for five years of Orr's services. Even I, lacking the least idea about financial or historical contexts, recognized the implications of the gigantic number. "We have gambled," ownership heir Bill Wirtz said. "We have placed our bet down, but at least we have gambled on a thoroughbred."

A thoroughbred with a bad knee of such scientific interest it appeared on *Nova*. A knee so bad MasterCard traced out the highlights of his career using the scars as a timeline. What possessed the Wirtz family, of all the living apostles of tightfistedness, to sign off on that record-breaking contract? On the one hand, give them credit for an audacious move. On the other, question everyone's judgment and blood alcohol level. Because, thoroughbred or not, a guy with a wrecked knee should come at a discount. Worse, the deal had PR nightmare written right above Orr's signature. Even the most bedazzled Hawks lifer remembered the team had dumped the legendary Bobby Hull—an ambulatory top-tier Hall of Famer—over less money just four years earlier.

The papers offered that low attendance may have motivated Chicago's move. Hawks fans increasingly declined the honor to watch the Hawks' put-'em-to-sleep, no-offense style, if style is the word for it. "Last year our power play was so bad that we used to talk about refusing the penalties," said Pit Martin.

Like ninety-nine percent of the country, I saw Orr in a Hawks uniform only via still photography. Where we lived, the local sportscasters led with video of high school football games and a round-up of prep scores long enough to fill the Book of Numbers. What time remained went to a clip montage of the Cubs or Bears or college football seasoned with whatever novelties had come over the network feed that day. A manager kicking dirt. A bobsled wipeout. Oh, hold on. A hockey fight.

RED HAIRED LIKE ME

7

Only hockey fans would make a defenseman with fourteen career goals and countless lost altercations their franchise's all-time most beloved player. Keith Magnuson supplanted Orr as my favorite at the same time all Hawks fans took him to heart.

Doing time as life's punching bag is a station anyone without an inheritance must pass to achieve anything in this world. Not to get too philosophical here, but I think Magnuson appealed in part because he was akin to a kind of mythic figure we love in movies, the Rocky Balboas, or maybe in his case the Wile E. Coyotes. People loved him not because he tried, but because he tried again.

It helped that Magnuson's winning personality came through even at a fan's remove. News stories of the time never passed on the chance to mention his Opie face and floppy hair, his loyalty, his ready smile. Whereas most guys with his resume projected an aura of danger or at least poor impulse control, he never registered as a classic scary goon. You get the feeling Magnuson dropping the mitts didn't inspire fear so much as weary resignation.

I could love Magnuson because I'd heard of Magnuson. Though he averaged about 1.5 goals per season, he made the highlights if any Hawk did, flailing away at all comers on the black-and-white TV. Magnuson swung like the Wirtzes paid him by the punch, the hit-to-miss ratio be damned, swung like a Little Rascal fighting Butch. The *Globe and Mail* offered the tale of the trainer's tape in 2003: ". . . a cracked cheek bone, three knee injuries involving surgery, a torn Achilles, two broken ankles, a dislocated elbow, three broken jaws, a broken vertebra, a broken wrist, a dislocated shoulder, three missing teeth, and more than 400 stitches."

Just three teeth?

Attention gets many pro jocks in trouble. Twitter and Instagram have been coke habit-level disasters for dozens of them. But scrutiny enhanced Magnuson's likability. Even spending a chunk of his Hawks tenure as an eligible bachelor did not expose him to scandal. Well, not the usual scandals.

The young hockey star relaxes on his custom-made bed—a white, vinyl coated dome with a round mattress inside and a chandelier. The bedspread is fake fur. The orange walls, black ceiling, and white shag rug [a sort of zebra pattern—KC] represent the colors of the Black Hawks.

The Hawk theme also carries through into the den. The large mural on the wall in the photo below depicts a hockey stick, a puck and a stylized ice rink. Again, the room is decorated in Black Hawk colors with black walls plus a black, red, and white supergraphic stripe running along the staircase walls.

In the accompanying photos, Magnuson lounges on the round bed in the requisite big-collared shirt, sweater, and plaid pants, an ensemble my mother dressed me in often. Magnuson worked it better, though in my defense that outfit is hard to pull off when you aren't old enough to grow sideburns.

The too-brief flashes of Magnuson versus the league failed to sustain my interest, however. I drifted away from the consumption of hockey even in its print forms. As I entered middle school, the faintest echoes of adulthood—as hard to detect as the emissions of pulsars, but there—awakened other interests that competed with sports. I had discovered writing and a predictable interest in the opposite sex, and also began a long obsession with music and became aware of money, to such an extent I took it upon myself to save my family from its financial straits by inventing . . . a successful board game. Exactly. Girls beat a path from my door.

For a time, hockey became a mere signifier, one of the countless bricks I used in the construction of a self I prayed others would find acceptable. Like new wave music and indie comics—both introduced to me by worldly peers a grade or two ahead—hockey did not fall far outside the mainstream. But it did dwell in a distant enough place to offer the illusion of a risk taken, particularly in a one-horse industrial town lousy with white people. It also carried that scent of injustice we feel when the popularity of a Real Thing falls short of what everyone else is into, an injustice I felt acutely when Ted Nugent fans threatened to beat me up because I knew the words to "Tainted Love."

My parents chose a good stretch of years to live outside of the Blackhawks' media reach. Though the team always made the come-one-come-all playoffs, first-round opponents swept them out of the postseason four seasons in a row. Going through that ordeal might have built my character, but on balance I don't regret a lack of Blackhawks-related memories of that era.

I do own relics. Years ago my friend J. P. (not Bordeleau) offered me a poster of the 1979–80 squad's team picture. Full color, with the schedule printed across the bottom and the number for SportsPhone across the top. Do you remember Sports-

Phone? Call for the daily Blackhawks report at 12:45 p.m. and interviews given in the hockey-player monotone. In defiance of laws against the destruction of culturally significant antiquities, J. P. otherwise planned to toss it and an equally handsome World Hockey Association poster with all the logos.

An irony: J. P. grew up in Elmhurst, the longtime Hawks enclave in the western suburbs. Neighbors of his hosted a few of the team's young call-ups, and J. P. spent time with the likes of Darcy Rota and Grant Mulvey. J. P. played Mulvey in ping pong and, he tells me, usually emerged victorious. I believe him. First, J. P. is mad for ping pong to such a degree it baffles his non-Chinese friends. Second, hockey skills and ping pong skills seem to have little overlap, except maybe in the case of goalies. As J. P. said:

> I guess I was more like fourteen or fifteen, and really only a few years younger than them at the time, but worlds away in looking like an athlete. I of course got a huge kick out of kicking the butt of a pro hockey player at the ping pong table. As I remember Grant didn't really know how to act. He just took the beating without saying a lot. Both those guys [Rota and Mulvey] are really nice guys. . . . When I was in my early to mid-thirties, after I had moved closer to Chicago, my nephew Jay played Little League baseball for a couple years around age ten or eleven. Turned out he was on the same team as Grant Mulvey's kid. For several games in the summer of 1992 or so, I coached first base and Grant coached third base.

The photo must be the last team picture to feature Mikita. There he is, seated front-row right. Arthur Wirtz sits at center, with mustachioed star Terry Ruskowski on the other side. Tony Esposito bookends Bill Wirtz and other members of the brass at right. A suited Magnuson stands smiling among the coaches. Once I mounted the poster, it hung on my wall for years. It creeps me out to think of the Wirtzes staring at some of the stuff that happened in that room. None of it impressed the players, I'm sure.

8

Deprived of direct exposure to hockey, I had a flirtation with soccer inspired by Pelé's time with the New York Cosmos. Soccer and hockey shared certain traits: back-and-forth action, putting an object in a goal, players with foreign names. Though inferior to hockey in all ways, soccer did have the virtue of being easier to play. You just needed a ball. In addition, I had neighbors who played it as effortlessly as my friends and I played basketball or baseball.

We called these neighbors the Laotians. My dad said they were Hmong, that legendary warrior people of Southeast Asia who had aided the U.S. during the Vietnam War. For all I know he made it up, like his old wives' tale about how salt cooled our food, a bit of malarkey I believed deep into my twenties. Several Hmong families lived in a four-unit building just off the playground at my then-home apartment complex. All were wiry, stoic, clearly dangerous, always smoking, and gifted in the masculine arts. We watched in admiration as the menfolk walked home with enormous carp pulled from the same water-filled old quarries where we struggled to hook bluegills.

My dad worked as the apartment complex's maintenance man. To the Hmong he was the guy who kept the stoves and refrigerators running and therefore worthy of their goodwill. Being both familiar and helpful, he occasionally served as their liaison to the American world, as when a group of the men slaughtered a goat in the trunk of an Oldsmobile. The neighbors, not understanding, involved the police. Dad mediated long enough to break the ice and gave way to the Hmong negotiators.

The adolescent Hmong, though never standoffish, stuck with each other. The younger ones had passable English and interacted with us. To be friendly, we gave them titles as nicknames. Li, maybe five years old, became Doctor Li. Pau, about the same age, became Professor Pau. They had good manners and no fear. Of all the creatures I have seen chase a squirrel, Li came the closest to catching one, because he dared to take the pursuit into a tree.

The older Hmong kids crossed over the cultural barrier for one activity: soccer. Any four of them could beat ten of us, even if they included Li or Pau in the quartet. Headers, back-kicks, fierce dribbling, majestic twenty-yard kicks that wobbled like knuckle-balls—we had no chance. It was worth getting trounced to see them work their game. After they had run us ragged, we stood and watched them take on one another.

For them it was like playing keep-away with a toddler. Mostly there was a lot of laughter, from us, too. We had nothing of our budding masculinity *invested* in soccer. None of us had even played a competitive game. Since we didn't understand the rules beyond no touching the ball with your hands, it meant less to our egos than even a gym-class game of Capture the Flag. No one staked bragging rights by stepping out on the field—we had no idea you called a soccer field a pitch—and no one felt inferior, or superior, to any of the other guys regardless of how the play went. It may have been one of the last moments of pure play in our lives. We already sensed—from all the other sports we played, from *Monopoly* games and racing our bikes and arm wrestling— the approach of an adulthood that asked us to live all areas of life in one arena or another, where the powers that be maintained a world that forced us to compete against friends as well as strangers, even in profound ways against people we loved.

RED MENACES

9

I don't remember much of my elementary- or middle-school scholarship, but somewhere in there English teachers assigned me research reports. The one on silkworms, for instance. My English teacher gave me the topic, drawn at random. Aware of my classmates' level of interest in cloth-spinning insect larva, I dreaded the oral report portion of the project, but I never complained, even to my interior self, because the guy who drew "make-up" out of the hat had it worse.

A different teacher allowed us to submit a list of topics for her to choose from. By then I had accumulated a wider range of interests. Rabbits, for instance, after burning through *Watership Down*, the first long novel I'd ever read; and genealogy, thanks to watching *Roots* with the rest of the country. I'm sure tornadoes and extraterrestrials made the list. Naturally, I put hockey first. It seemed clever, a chance to read books I read on my own already and get school credit for it.

The teacher spared herself the umpteenth male student report on sports by spinning off hockey into the history of ice skating. It was a shocking disappointment, not only because I lost a way to work Bobby Orr into my project, but because ice skating as a topic seemed both vast— that is, a lot of work—and boring. As odd as it sounds, I had only a vague notion that ice skating connected to hockey. Okay, I knew the players skated. But I had never contemplated the skill itself, or the necessity of being good at it, at least not as much as I'd thought about slap shots and fighting and impenetrable Gallic pronunciations. Ice skating. For me the phrase conjured a mental image of figure skaters. No offense, I loved Dorothy Hamill as much as the next guy, but I had no interest in the scholarship of a topic soaked in girliness.

While cribbing from Britannica, I discovered ice skating had its own history, one accompanied by quaint drawings of Dutchpersons gliding on canals. I liked history. I could write a history report. The teacher, a pleasant and seen-it-all veteran of the profession, added a twist. One day in class, she defined the word *bibliography* and then ordered us to provide one, stressing that the books and magazine articles had to (1) exist and (2) contribute to the writing of the paper. I and most of my classmates turned in a report with a bibliography that showed our near-total ignorance of the concept. The rest either blew off the back matter or didn't turn in a paper in the first place.

I delved into the mysteries of skating. Thanks to Catholic school, I accepted that the Church's saints had discovered or invented everything, a level of prodigiousness unmatched until twentieth-century Soviets insisted the Wright brothers had robbed Russian aviators of credit for manned flight. Sure enough, medieval ice skating got a boost, though admittedly not its start, from St. Lidwina, a Dutch seer and healer known for never eating or sleeping, and for having body parts steadily fall off or out—this included her intestines—after a fall on the ice.

I don't remember what else went into the report. I do recall overwriting it by many pages, a vice that exhausted my instructors at all subsequent levels, in fact overwriting to such a degree that I shattered the page count and an adequate level of extra credit before I could get to a section on the Blackhawks. I made up for that with a ballpoint-pen-on-Mead drawing of hockey action, to go with my illustrations of Dutch children and (I hope) St. Lidwina losing an arm.

Few book reports prepare us for life. Delving into the history of ice skating was different. Not because I got a better than usual grade. Poor spelling and my chimp-with-a-tremor penmanship undid any goodwill earned by my enthusiasm. The report was in my recent past when the 1980 Winter Olympic Games made everyone around me interested in hockey.

● Jingoism unites, whatever else you can say about it, and in my neighborhood the transplants and bandwagon jumpers covered up their Cardinals pennants and Cowboys T-shirts and Dr. J school folders to support Team USA as one. That year's Olympic hockey team represented a great rarity in our culture: the chance to cheer on the United States as an underdog. It takes no gift for sociological insight to see why Americans felt like one. The country had been through a rough ten years, and flipping to a new decade hadn't improved things, with the hostages in Iran and inflation and, personally speaking, having to change clothes for gym class.

Furthermore, as everyone loved to point out, the Soviets had a team of professionals, whereas the U.S. sent out plucky college students and other greenhorns, an unconscionable disadvantage for us, yea, an affront to the ethics of sportsmanship, this being the era before Kobe Bryant Globetrottered all over starstruck Angolans. It was one with having to compete for world supremacy against a country that somehow scared us despite being ruled by geriatric spies and drunk yokels and suffering from an economic depression that had lasted longer than *Days of Our Lives*.

Only two things threatened to distract me from this long-awaited reunion with my beloved sport: a new Cheap Trick album (*Dream Police*) and chickenpox.

And what chickenpox. The virus seemed to amplify as it passed through each of my sisters. I don't remember any of them suffering. Erin, the youngest and then a toddler, seemed to sleep through the entire period of infection. But I managed to catch a rib-rattling respiratory illness on top of chickenpox, meaning I coughed and sneezed and shivered while covered with itchy blisters my mother swore would leave me disfigured if I dared to scratch them. I sought relief in the shower, not the worst solution, given I had not quite dropped the indifference to hygiene found among grade-school-aged boys.

I had forgotten a lot about hockey since the NHL's exile. The intricacies of icing and offsides came back to me in bits and pieces, however, and I understood enough of what was going on to try to impress my sisters and my dog with my knowledge. I did wonder about the lack of fighting. There didn't even seem to be that much pushing and shoving. Did the TV network cut those parts out? Did Sweden and Norway share Switzerland's commitment to nonviolent neutrality? I had no idea.

The U.S. beat West Germany on my birthday, a victory I experienced via highlights, either because I missed the game in a daze or because ABC preferred to show figure skating. Quarantine also meant I missed cheering on the team with noisy friends who might be interested to hear the history of the boot skate during intermission. But no complaints. Hockey provided one of the few things engrossing enough to make me forget I looked monstrous.

A game against the Soviets seemed predestined, the culmination of thirty-some years of cold war and the dreams of ABC Sports execs. Pop and political culture had instilled in me a casual loathing of commies. My temperament made it hard for me to loathe anything more than casually, but to keep up appearances in moments of weak good nature I too professed to see the Soviets as another manifestation of whatever malevolent force animated the world's evils. It didn't help that I had grown up in places where people sincerely connected the Soviet Union to fluoridation and/or rock music and, worse, remained eager to evangelize on their beliefs. Small towns buzz with conspiracy. Even my mom, a woman neither given to nor patient with imagination, could lay down the exhaustive details of a half-dozen intrigues related to the Kennedy assassination, or alternately how JFK still lived on a secret upper floor of a Dallas hospital.

The Olympics had always floated its yacht on the tarry waters of tribalism rather than its professed admiration for the glories of amateur sport. As a showdown with the Soviets became more likely, everyone from ABC to flea-market hucksters selling USA belt buckles wanted a piece of the action. The Americans went into the game very much able to lose. America, however, did not. If Team USA won, then it was glory and fireworks. If Team USA lost, everyone could complain that the Soviets and their system of paid amateurism had rigged the game in their favor.

I sound unpatriotic now, and acted it then, I'm afraid. The chickenpox had progressed to itchy scabs, but my respiratory issues remained severe, and I dozed off again and again. It's possible the Americans' impossible second goal, with one tick left on the clock, returned me to life. Scoring at 19:59, in any hockey game, seems like an omen on a par with a comet killing an albatross. I did make it back to consciousness for the end of the game and the handshake—for some reason I was surprised Russians had red hair. My dad, never one to hoot in victory, expressed one of his happier superlatives, "Well, how about that?" or maybe, "I'll be damned."

For my father it was ninety minutes of taped-delayed entertainment, then off to get rid of the garbage and clean up the mess the dog had made. I learned well. Years later, after Kane's Cup winner, I took fifteen minutes to be stunned, watched Jeremy Roenick cry, answered a couple of congratulatory phone calls from friends, and went back to work on whatever assignment I had in progress. At some point after midnight I sighed and thought, Man, I wish a Stanley Cup could change my life.

No longer contagious, I returned to school and friends, rehashed hockey matters with those who cared, and answered questions about chickenpox. By that point, the U.S. had beaten Finland for the gold medal, and I'd forgotten the history of ice skating in favor of whatever trivia I'd picked up about Team USA from *Sports Illustrated*. It's the first time I can remember large numbers of peers having any enthusiasm for hockey, maybe for one of my obsessions, period.

THE MASCULINE MYSTIQUE

10

People in nowhere towns, deprived of so much else, often got bitching early cable systems. In 1980, I had never been to an art museum, but I had seen a Residents video because the place I lived was an original testing ground for MTV. Thanks to the USA Network, I also had access to broadcast hockey again. Very few games, but it gave me hope one would be on while I flipped the channels, and my study of *TV Guide* included a regular check to see if the Blackhawks made the schedule. Inevitably, watching games progressed into a living room roll-on-the-floor brawl with whatever friend was over, and ended with one or both of my parents threatening a lot worse than two minutes in the box.

We had no idea how cheap-ass the telecast looked, no inkling that the hosts of a pro sporting event should light their rink with more than a sixty-watt bulb. If the league had little control over the look of the broadcasts, or who bid on the games, you get the feeling the owners didn't much care about the dinginess of their product, that as a cabal they hadn't much evolved from the days when Canadiens execs declined to allow Habs games on the wireless, and thereby handed over an entire nation's beating heart to the Maple Leafs.

• My dad took a job a couple of hours away in the Chicago suburbs. For a time he would visit us on weekends or every other weekend. No doubt he missed his wife and children. But he married at twenty and became a father a month after turning twenty-one. Maybe he didn't mind the respite. When the school year ended, he returned with the moving truck. I contemplated being the new kid in class for the seventh or eighth time in my life but also looked forward to a huge slate of Cubs and White Sox games on free TV in the summer, and Blackhawks road games in the winter.

Baseball came through. The Hawks, though—I have no idea what fly-by-night operation partnered with the Wirtz family in those days. Games, though only away games, did make it to television. I swear I saw a few at friends' houses, and I used to ask my folks to drop me on the downtown main drag, ostensibly so I could go to the used book store, but also because it gave me the chance to watch East Coast games through the window of a local bar.

Even if the Wirtzes had allowed every game on free TV, an impossible hypothetical, I was doomed to limited contact. I lived in a house with two TV-watching parents and three younger sisters who, in addition to having their own favorite shows, viewed their *Purple Rain* tape five times a week. Plus, the one way in the world to piss off my grandmother was to ask her to miss *Hunter* on Saturday nights.

Thus, the radio.

Television, while inferior to seeing a game live, at least offers a simulacrum of hockey. Trust me, tune in enough and you learn to track the puck. It's just a matter of watching the players' reactions to it. Meanwhile, the cameras and replays treat you to the goals and chances, to the sweetest passes and the most devastating checks. On top of that, hockey is amazingly photogenic. For whatever reason—the gorgeous uniforms over bodies made modular by pads, the grace forced on the athletes by making them move on blades, a background white enough for a *Vogue* shoot—it outclasses all of the other major sports for aesthetics. Only pro basketball even competes.

The wireless, though. Jesus. Nick Hornby wrote, "Radio football is football reduced to its lowest common denominator." This truism also applies to ice hockey, a much faster game where part of the visceral pleasure of spectating arises from physical contact. Did a check send a guy flying? Or crush him into the boards? Or was it a hip upending him at center ice?

In hockey, less visual stimuli means no adrenalin, no dopamine, no ability to feel along with a player who drones "It's an emotional game" after cheap-shotting an opponent. On the radio the ups-and-downs of the game come across as a flatline, hockey on Prozac, a pleasant enough distraction but at its core purely informational. Hockey on the radio is like watching a kiss. Sure, some basic information gets conveyed. But you miss out on what matters. Hatred for the Blues, no matter how much a constant in your life, cannot burst into the white-hot flame that brings us catharsis, and gives our lives meaning.

There's a reason we as a civilization ditched oral storytelling. But hockey, with me and I suspect with Hornby if circumstances force him to listen to Arsenal on the radio, becomes worse than unsatisfying. It's agonizing. You cannot call upon the gods when the other team puts together a breakaway. You cannot bitch in a satisfyingly informed way that Corey Crawford should've stopped the fifty-footer that scooted beneath his stick. Thus are we deprived of enjoying one of the most liberating, primal moments allowed us by an uncaring universe: demanding that the goalie be pulled mid-game.

Hockey on the radio works on the same principle as a horror film that refuses to show the monster. When Dallas descends into the tunnels of his ship in *Alien,* we know the creature is even more dangerous than before, and that's saying something because fifteen minutes earlier it exploded out of a guy's chest. The other members of the crew trace Dallas's progress with a tracking device that shows moving forms as dots on a grid. In other words, a machine as primitive to futuristic space workers as radio is to us. Their suspense becomes palpable because they can *hear* Dallas but not see him. Once a second dot pops up and heads toward Dallas—xenomorph on the breakaway—the crewmembers experience that horrible feeling of impending misfortune/ doom mixed with a lack of information about what's happening.

Furthermore, radio takes away our personal ability to affect the game. Hockey, especially postseason hockey, returns me to a mindset common to medieval peasants. If only I wear this bone of a hanged man, the Hawks penalty kill will hang on. Our rational selves realize this is ridiculous. Did the 2013 Hawks engrave my name on the Cup for doing all of the above and saving them from the Bruins? Of course not. In the moment, though, it seemed almost reasonable that my nervous nose scratching in a Los Angeles apartment triggered a butterfly effect that made Zdeno Chára overskate a puck thousands of miles away.

Yet radio re-addicted me to hockey. Or, rather, Pat Foley did. I became an immediate and dedicated fan. One of the first things I did when I finally attended a Hawks game was find Foley with my mini-binoculars. The team's shabby treatment of him in the 2000s initiated my own "final" break with the pathetic franchise the Hawks had become.

Foley was a revelation. Never before had I heard an announcer drop that kind of energy on regular play-by-play. But his true genius was the way he transcended any need for actual language.

Let's try a thought experiment. In our hypothetical, Foley loses a bet on the golf course and must call a game using only the words *watermelon* and *cantaloupe*. He also has to say them in that order, over and over, watermelon-cantaloupe-watermelon-cantaloupe.

Listeners would lose nothing from Foley's game call. His use of tone, inflection, energy, and timber in and of itself is a complex linguistic system akin to the Silbo Gomero whistling language of the Canary Islands, one capable of expressing both the range of hockey-related human emotions (that is, all of them) and the complexities of the power play. In fact, within the parameters of our bet, he renders even watermelon and cantaloupe superfluous. An imaginary snippet of play-by-play:

```
watermelon-cantaloupe . . . waterrrrmelon, waaa-no,
cantaloupe, watermelon, cantaLOUPE-WATER-WATER-
MELON-CANTALOUUUUUUUUUUUUUPPPPPPPE
[horn sounds]
```

In time Foley became my strongest link to the Hawks, or second strongest, if you count all the Hawks-themed clothing I owned. Announcers are never the face of a functional franchise, but they nonetheless provide the continuity that a team can never sustain because of player turnover.

If proximity and Foley encouraged my return to active hockey fandom, the usual adolescent confusions surrounding manhood cemented it. Soccer just didn't bring the macho posturing that, however ridiculous, traps the teenaged male heart. I liked soccer. It's just I found little to emulate in the way of what I imagined to be manly behavior. I blamed the game, not those who played it, because I knew better. Remember, my main contact with soccer came via Laotian kids no one considered wimpy in the least. We respected their ability to live with very little, to look carved from stone even when smiling, and to eat meat butchered in their car a half hour earlier.

Hockey offered innumerable role models for forming a proper masculine identity, or what I considered a proper masculine identity. My rabbi was Al Secord. He was the player type beloved of adolescent males of all ages: the ass-kicker who scored goals. In 1981–82, Big Al spent over three hundred minutes in the box while putting forty-four goals in the net. The next season he became the first Hawk since Bobby Hull to top fifty goals (fifty-four, with 180 penalty minutes).

Here was a man. As a teen, Secord fought fires. "The Ministry of Natural Resources would fly us out to fire sites in de Havilland Otters and Beavers and occasionally in helicopters," he told the Toronto *Star*. He added manfully, "I'd like to be a bush pilot."

Instead, he became a commercial pilot for American Airlines. Is there any more traditionally masculine occupation than pilot? Not in the children's books I see.

For a skinny, arty dope trying to figure out manhood, Secord seemed like Heracles and Achilles, like Steve Austin and Rocky Balboa.

The stories just kept on coming. Coach Orval Tessier restricted Big Al's over-the-top weightlifting regimen. Big Al tried boxing as an amateur in Canada. He clubbed accursed North Stars tough guy Dino Ciccarelli to the ice with his stick. The legion of non–North Stars fans despised Dino so much that to this day they accuse him of taking a dive. He even broke the chains on the relatively civilized confines of international hockey when he floored Swiss star Jakob Koelliker as a member of Team Canada in 1987. "It was the left hand that did the job," Secord said. He had punched Koelliker on the way to the penalty box.

Hellenic glory sheened even his injuries:

Secord's right leg had been driven up into his hip. The muscles surrounding the joint between the leg and the hip became stretched to their full extent and eventually began to tear with each additional stride. Eventually, the muscles in the surrounding area, which were beginning to compensate for the damaged muscles of the joint, also began to deteriorate under the strain.

It's more accurate to say Secord represented an ideal. After all, rather than hitting the weights and my fellow man, I remained a skinny, arty dope with weak ankles. Following Secord's exploits clued me in to what I wished to be, *wish* being the operative word, for even in the unwise years of my young adulthood I had enough self-awareness to see I had nothing in common with Al Secord, except that I've flown American Airlines.

Jokes aside, and sitting here decades later, I still feel a shadow of the same inadequacy. Not enough to keep me up nights. I'm at an age where I've made a melancholy peace with the idea I won't fight crime or land on Mars. But the regret lingers. I mean, who knew teenagers fought fires? But even if I'd known, I lacked the imagination to run away to Ontario to do it. At that young age, I had no idea that life offered those kinds of possibilities, that it offered possibilities at all, beyond mere survival. The shortage of moxie to, I don't know, become a hockey player-slash-pilot, to fearlessly lay the lumber on Dino Ciccarelli (something I wanted to do many times)—that's on me. I feel it acutely, in the maudlin way common to middle-aged American men. At times, I wish I remained in the featureless box of my youthful ignorance. If adventure and many of the world's pleasures seemed unattainable, at least I could kid myself with *some day*.

Then I cheer up and think, Just produce a piece of writing like *Death of a Salesman*, and Salma Hayek will marry you.

11

Somewhere in there I began an unremarkable college career. In hindsight, I'm lucky to have a degree from a major university. I skipped the better part of my sophomore year of high school, undone by social anxiety and a lack of interest in any subject unrelated to writing or history. I lacked even the basic truancy skills that made ditching so memorable for my cousins and my less respectable friends. They bummed around or smoked weed. I waited for my parents to leave for work, let myself into the house, and wrote books or practiced on the left-handed guitar my mom bought me at a thrift store.

Later, when my parents moved me to the suburbs and the nearby prep school, I walked into a room to take the ACT without the least idea of what awaited me. Not only did I not prepare; I didn't know people took classes to prepare. I thought you were *supposed* to take the test cold, to offer university administrators a pure measurement of what you had learned all those years. No one told me I could retake the test senior year, either.

Thus I ended up at community college, a great disappointment to my mother and myself, though at least not a financial burden. I put myself through with a combination of part-time jobs, work study, and acting (truly an accurate verb) as advertising manager of the student newspaper. I also made enough to afford to gas up a succession of beaters, including a purple Cadillac the size of a Zamboni—same gas mileage, too. The scorned ex-girlfriend of the previous owner gave it real street cred. She had spider-webbed the passenger-side corner of the windshield with a revolver butt.

Hockey, like the provenance of a thirdhand Cadillac, has a way to be simultaneously appalling and hilarious. I know that, as a civilized human being, I am supposed to tsk-tsk the fact that Secord clocked Koelliker on the way to the penalty box. In other contexts, a cheap shot like that would draw censure. That it provided a testosterone buzz and inspiration to several thousand males, many older than me, is, if not understandable or forgivable, at least comprehensible. Haven't we all wanted to slug a persistent nuisance at our workplace?

Yet, with my intellect awakened by college, I began to see the violent, dumbass side of hockey as theoretically objectionable. To cope, I laughed off hockey's on-ice excesses as a way to safeguard myself against the unmanly thought that pounding another human being was a less-than-ethical method of conflict resolution. Necessary, sure. Hockey, like all workplaces, had its code of behaviors. The long list of unwritten rules made the warning "Violence begets more violence" about as effective a motto as "Please clean your coffee cup." Koelliker, after all, had teed off on Secord three times before Big Al sent him to Fist City. You have to deter that sort of thing, I told myself. Grody coffee cups get dropped "by accident" for similar reasons.

Still, for the first time I found it difficult to divorce myself from the knowledge that, Dino Ciccarelli notwithstanding, I was watching human beings. They bruised, they broke, and they bled—more so than we realized then. Laughing off the pains they inflicted on one another sounds heartless in hindsight. To say nothing of chuckling (while shaking our heads) that so-and-so played the better part of a postseason with a collapsed spleen or broken foot or some other astonishing nonsense.

I thought of hockey excess in the way I thought of the crazy behavior of my relatives. You look at these people and want to say: It's a bad idea to eat that much hashish. To choose two cases of beer over life jackets when packing the fishing boat for a day on Lake Michigan. To insult the girlfriend of a guy named Earthquake. To set off fireworks in the car.

Yet, what's the alternative to laughing? Cousins and uncles do crazy shit. It's why we have cousins and uncles. And there's no stopping them. They have free will. If Koelliker insisted on slugging Al Secord and Secord took the unsporting step of hitting him while en route to the box, you had to laugh and say, "That's hockey," because you couldn't embrace the game without allowing for dumbassery that, under ordinary circumstances, would trouble your conscience or, worse, excite you. Hockey's extremes could make me laugh or shake with fury. I preferred to laugh, but more uneasily as time went by.

● Growing up, elders gave me two firm warnings about the Chicago Stadium. One, fights continually raged in the stands. Two, rats the size of badgers prowled everywhere. Though I'd never see either since black people would kill me as I traveled through the near West Side to the game.

I survived the commute through the West Side and regularly exited the building without bubonic plague or a black eye. I never saw any kind of rodent. Other than some pushing and shoving, and that infrequent, I saw very little violence off the ice. Compare that to Wrigley Field. Before it became a beer garden in the mid-nineties, I never sat in the bleachers without seeing shoving matches—if not a donnybrook between rival packs of tour-bus passengers—and as for the young women in Cubby blue vomiting into garbage cans, the less said the better.

The Stadium opened on Madison Street in 1929. A portentous year: future Hawks owner William Wadsworth Wirtz entered this world of sorrow in October. The Wirtzes had no stake in pro hockey in those days. The team belonged to Frederic McLaughlin, a coffee magnate who also served as general manager and went by the name of the Major, after his rank in the 333rd Machine Gun "Black Hawk" Regiment during the Great War. McLaughlin would go on to a mostly disastrous career as an executive and earn a memorable elegy from Maple Leafs owner Conn Smythe: "Where hockey was concerned . . . [he was] perhaps the biggest nut I met in my entire life."

In a 1928–29 season renowned for defense—120 of the 220 NHL games ended in a shutout—the Hawks went over a lunar month without scoring. They managed only thirty-three total goals in forty-four games. To add insult to injury, bad ice and scheduling problems forced the team out of the Chicago Coliseum, the team's home in the pre-Stadium era, in January. The Hawks played the rest of their home games in Detroit and even further along the stagecoach route in Fort Erie, Ontario.

The team became tenants at the Stadium the next season. The barn accommodated over seventeen thousand people—a lot more when McLaughlin bribed the fire marshal. James E. Norris, a Chicago millionaire and McLaughlin's neighbor, owned a piece of the building. Soon he added control of Madison Square Garden to his holdings. Landlord status gave him influence over both the Hawks and New York Americans, the forerunners of the Rangers. Money loaned to Boston meant he had a say in the Bruins, too. League poohbahs then allowed Norris to keep these deals in place after he bought the Detroit Cougars, the forerunners of the Red Wings, in 1932.

Historians will note this arrangement set the tone for eighty-plus years of ethical management in the NHL. I note it because the shady behavior of ownership might connect to another myth: that the Stadium's concrete served as the final resting place of gangland figures from the Prohibition years. Every time I walked by the demolition site in the nineties, I expected to see an avalanche of bones. A mobster burial ground would have explained many events in team history.

Cleverer minds have written about the Stadium's charms. Other than the noise—a tremendous sound when the place got rocking—the charms seem as exaggerated as the rodent life. It was a much better place to stand than the current building. Since that's all I could afford to do, nights along the railing at the opposite end from the organ form my memories. When work or other obstacles allowed, I arrived early to see the skate-around and hear the random cries of "[Star player] sucks." When possible, I planted myself at the rail and prepared to remain there for three hours. In future years, when the Hawks became a hot ticket and standing room turned into a mosh pit, that rail almost cut me in half four or five times. But at first there was plenty of space. The scoreboard hid the far end, a less than ideal situation; but you stood directly above the other goal.

I thought I'd have to fight for my choice spot, all the more so since, being fairly tall and the owner of a giant Germanic head, I further obstructed an already obstructed view. At times it made me so self-conscious I gave up the rail after a period or two. Mostly two. I told myself it was only fair. I could see plenty from behind people. Once off the rail I could also go to the bathroom. Few of my companions shared my willingness to be pinned to the rail, so once I gave over my spot, I drifted up that staircase-to-nowhere in the corner set aside as a sanctuary for latecomers and demophobes, and rejoined them.

Holding that spot kept me from spending too much of my tuition money on beer and, relatedly, from spending too much time waiting in lines in the bathroom. It also gave me a chance to learn about hockey. It was like watching through a Skycam. I saw how the players tracked one another, the whiplash forced on them by turnovers and clearing passes, the utter defenselessness of a goaltender as an odd-man rush bore down on him.

Once, while watching a game on TV in college, I said something along the lines of, "I wish they'd run that play more." One of my roommates replied, "They have *plays*?" I laughed, knowingly rather than derisively. It had taken me years to realize hockey was not a wholly improvisational illustration of chaos, on a par with an Easter egg hunt for preschoolers. Learning to *see* became unbearably exciting, just as learning to think—or what passed for thinking with me—had seized me by the collar in college. I dived into the butterfly style and C. Wright Mills, for better or for worse, with the same eagerness.

Sports knowledge, plus growing up with a garbage pail for a brain, began to pay off. Carrying the Blackhawks in my back pocket let me connect with the younger guys at the newspapers where I covered meetings and along the rail at the Stadium, with random coworkers and the male kin of female friends.

For all that sports can teach us about teamwork and commitment and all the rest, for males its most important function is that it provides an essential vocabulary for dealing with one another. Like denying our emotions, it starts young in us. My whole childhood, it seemed as if I started every September at a new school. Knowing how to throw/shoot/kick a ball, and how to talk about the guys who did it professionally, provided me with more social benefits than did long division.

I'm not saying childhood should be this way, or that one cannot find other common ground—woodworking, Boy Scouts, whatever. It's just that, in my experience, the ability to catch a batted ball and talk about sports let me enter the varied societies we navigate from the playground onward. It also warped me, of course. Despite knowing better, I still look with suspicion on any grown American male who cannot throw a baseball or take a jump shot, a blatant hypocrisy, as the average Canadian or Russian would weep at the sight of me on ice skates.

Hockey talk gets me through wedding receptions, children's birthday parties, social events, unwanted conversations with drunks on the train, and work. Even when chatting with some diehard fan of an enemy team, the conversation remains civil. In part that's because of societal rules that frown on screaming matches at bar mitzvahs. But in part it's because the other guy is just as relieved as I am to find a way to endure whatever purgatory demanded by family or social or romantic loyalty. These discussions become more valued as we age, for the simple reason they are fewer and farther between. They provide us with a medium for expressing emotion that's vital to our health. Not incidentally, it also allows us to share a wealth of lovingly cultivated knowledge that, for many of us, is our only claim to expertise in anything.

MOUNT ORVAL

12

The 1984–85 season began with hope. The Black-hawks had parlayed their high draft picks into players that ranged from future Hall of Famers like Denis Savard to All-Stars like Doug Wilson to Calder Trophy winner Steve Larmer to a variety of useful and more-than-useful pieces like Steve Ludzik, Troy Murray, and Darryl Sutter. Add to that a rookie phenom (Ed Olczyk), the tough guy duo of Secord and Behn Wilson, and Murray Bannerman in goal. Behind the bench smoldered Orval Tessier, aka Mt. Orval, still around after proclaiming his team needed "heart transplants" during a grueling 1983 conference finals loss to the Edmonton Oilers.

Once mere schedule filler, like the Gin Blossoms at a throwback rock festival, the Hawks showed more promise than they had in ages. Tessier had already worked one miracle: getting the Blackhawks noticed by *Sports Illustrated*. Described as a "plain-looking pudgy man whose moon-face is framed by a double chin and a receding hairline" and who "looks like the guy who comes to fix the furnace," Tessier stressed defense and insisted on discipline, a phrase that in hockeyspeak meant not fighting at every opportunity. It was quite a change for the Hawks, and not altogether popular. Pre-Orval, the Hawks had played the style 1980s hockey fans dreamed of:

wild flourishes and mad rushes on offense, grabbing and shoving and punching the rest of the time. Discipline sounded not so much like a style than as a way to punish spectators.

Success and personality vaulted the Hawks into the regular rotation on the local sports highlights. Scenes of Tessier's red-faced tantrums interspersed with Savard's spin-moves and Doug Wilson's slap shot were sports anchor catnip. It helped that Tessier came across as sound rather than fury, a colorful uncle instead of a tyrant.

Yet, even with all the virtues the Hawks put out on the ice, no one believed they posed a threat to the Edmonton Oilers. It was impossible to believe anyone could beat Edmonton. Like all fans, I let loyalty immunize me against common sense, and I believed in my team. Not that I considered them better than the Oilers. But it was an NHL tradition for an elite team to miss the Finals while a six- or seven-seed burned through the postseason. A few breaks, and an upset of the Oilers in the early rounds, and the Hawks could be that year's blessed pretender.

The Hawks emerged from the annual disaster of the circus trip around .500 and worked their way solidly above break-even in the next few games. Then, from mid-December through early February, they seemed unable to beat any team except Toronto and Minnesota. The Hawks had no franchise on the accomplishment. The Leafs lost fifty-two games that season. Management further undercut the team's entertainment value by dismissing Tessier. With the Super Bowl–bound Bears dominating all media, the Hawks went back to fighting on the highlights, when they made it at all. They also installed head-coaching stunt double Bob Pulford for his third go-round at the job.

That was the season Wayne Gretzky scored 208 points and achieved the rare level of sports heroism where the league changes the rulebook to stop one player. The rest of the team played like an icebound Harlem Globetrotters while revolution-izing the game. The Hawks' road to a title, like everyone's road to a title, went past the Oilers, a team no one expected to lose, maybe ever again.

Chicago and Edmonton both swept through the first round. The Oilers then eliminated Winnipeg in four while the Hawks needed that many overtimes to take the last two of the last three games from the sorry North Stars. But we felt heartened. Hawks fans knew the tough series was a crucible. Our heroes had be-come grind-it-out, want-it-more winners. A little luck would be needed, but—

The Oilers hung an 11-2 loss on the Hawks to open the confer-ence finals. Did Jarri Kurri score from a stepladder? Did Grant Fuhr do the confetti-in-the-bucket trick with the audience? A co-worker invited me to watch a pirated satellite broadcast of the game. I had to work, thank God. The Hawks evened things up by taking two games at the Stadium. I drove out an entire tank of gas listening to the Hawks score eight goals in the second game. At one point in the drive, I ended up on an expressway—I have no idea what state it was in—and asked a gas station attendant for directions I was too stressed out to comprehend. By the time the series ended, Edmonton had scored forty-four goals in six games, and gone into double digits twice.

I watched all I could of that year's Stanley Cup on ESPN, con-tent to see Gretzky, Messier, Coffey, and the rest of these titans sans rooting interest. The experience lacked spice, but I was thrilled to see a sustained blast of elite hockey. At the time I had no inkling I'd ever see Wayne Gretzky play in person. If the idea ever crossed my mind, I'm sure I dismissed it as another of life's impossibilities, right up there with becoming a swashbuckling archaeologist.

Though pained by the massacre, I kept the faith. NHL history dictated that even the Oilers would bow out early once or twice in the postseason. On that day, the door would open for my team.

Sure enough, Calgary upset Edmonton the next spring. By the time it happened, the thoroughly crap Leafs had swept the Hawks. I vowed that I would never support them again. The next twenty-five seasons ended with that same pathetic promise to myself.

IT'S A SHAME ABOUT DAVE

13

There's a cliché that a would-be writer has to write a million bad words before any good ones start to flow. Lacking role models, industry contacts, innate gifts, knowledge of publishing, or any other legs up, I needed three million. I knocked out a few hundred thousand while indifferently training for technical writing, and journalism, and public relations—that is, a living—while hoping I had enough talent to make it as a bigger-than-life Literary Figure.

For instance, while scanning *Writer's Digest* or one of the related digests of literary delusion, I saw an ad from a publisher soliciting a series of supernatural mysteries. Suddenly, my encyclopedic knowledge of ancient astronauts had a commercial outlet. I went to work. Outlines for novels in the series. Long story arcs that would carry through from book to book. Character sketches paper-clipped to index cards crammed with personality traits and backstory written in my five-point handwriting.

And, longest of all, lists of the supernatural beings and junk science I had encountered over the years. Knowing I had to outrace a thousand other amateurs who wanted to avoid real jobs, I came up with a series built around a pair of investigators who investigated monsters like Bigfoot, urban myths like the Mattoon Gasser, and various exotic homicides. For maximum marketability—because I'd read it in a bogus How to Write a Bestseller article—I made the protagonists a woman and a man. The woman was a psychologist. The man was a former hockey player. I had only a vague idea about how he made a living as an investigator. This was the era before a player retired with millions. Having never had money, I had no feel for writing a billionaire playboy protagonist, so I stuck with what I thought I knew. One of the first books had the pair investigating a ghost trying to kill a French-Canadian minor leaguer. The male investigator, naturally, went undercover by joining the team. You get the idea. I had more postage stamps than sense and sent my packet of materials to the address in the ad. It will surprise you that I never heard back.

Inventing narratives kept my inner life busy during dull workdays and long car rides to classes or zoning board meetings. More importantly, storytelling provided a strategy, however flawed, for making sense of a chaotic outer life that swirled with work, stress, uncertainty, and the hungers that afflict young men.

Inevitably, I used narrative to try to gain the illusion of control over one of my main sources of anxiety.

One of my favorite hoarded relics is a copy of the *Tribune Sunday Magazine* dated March 24, 1991. The cover shows Blackhawks defenseman Dave Manson looking at the camera lens with two black eyes. "Tough Guy, Tough Game," the headline inside the magazine read. In the story, longtime *Trib* columnist Bob Verdi captured the combination of promise and lunacy that to that point had defined Manson's career.

Standing six-two, Manson seemed enormous for his time. He brought a Secord-esque mix of scoring acumen (fifty-four points in 1988–89 and an All-Star selection the next season) and, to put it mildly, a willingness to mix it up. Fans appreciated the goals, but they loved the "Charlie" Manson persona that Dave himself professed to despise. Not to say the man deserved to share the name with a murderous cult leader. But Manson went beyond the pale at times. Biting the finger of old sparring partner Scott Stevens, for example, an event that always makes internet list-cicles like "14 Greatest Hockey Biting Incidents." No other sport can claim so many biting incidents that you can argue over which ones to include.

Manson reached the dubious acme of his legend in a game against the Leafs on December 23, 1989. A five-on-five death match broke out at the end of the first period. After Hawks captain Dirk Graham got into a scuffle, the game went off the rails when Denis Savard, heretofore someone who only raised a fist if it held a cigarette, socked Leafs star Gary Leeman, and for a brief time Leeman socked back. Together these guys may have weighed three hundred pounds, and for Savard, at least, it marked his first fighting misconduct since arriving in the NHL. Minutes later, the two pacifists, perhaps having had enough, re-engaged with a center ice staredown while their teammates slugged it out. The refs tag-teamed Manson off the ice and into the tunnel, or so went their report. Manson then turned around and made a sort of aborted flying leap into the Savard-Leeman dance. En route he "bumped" the linesman by kicking his feet out from under him.

Manson earned a nigh-unheard-of triple-game misconduct. The league ignored his claim that he never left the ice and added a thirteen-game suspension. "The problem was that our guys were outnumbered," Manson explained. People called him a lot of things, but bad teammate was not on the list.

Manson possessed an integrity—I use the word sincerely, if uncomfortably—lacking in merely dirty players like Ulf Samuelsson. Samuelsson dished cheap-shots on the down low. When caught, he often looked incredulous. Manson, on the other hand, often didn't seem to care if the ref saw him or not, didn't always seem aware that refs officiated NHL games. That's not to say Manson failed to get away with his share of chippy play. Just that feigned outrage held no appeal for him. Fans appreciate it when they don't have to defend a hypocrite.

Had Manson come into the league without high expectations he might have joined Magnuson on the list of Hawks folk heroes. The Hawks, alas, drafted Manson in the first round, and talked up his scoring as well as his toughness. Though he delivered on both counts for a while, Manson, unlike Secord, faced boos for his transgressions, for his entire game, really. His defense tended toward the adventurous. He had problems choosing the right moment for his thundering slap shot. A majority of the three-hundred-plus minutes he spent in the box every season came on dumb penalties. His suspensions, when not related to biting or attempts to injure others too often were of the no-brain(er) kind, for instance that bad habit of "bumping" referees.

Verdi, assisted by Manson, summed up the enigma:

He does not get paid $300,000 a year by the Blackhawks to sit in a penalty box. He is gainfully employed by this Chicago team that thinks of itself as the NHL's best because he could be, should be and frequently is a rather accomplished hockey player, able to fulfill any number of useful functions.

"And that's what I want to be, what I want to be known as, a complete hockey player," Manson says. "I'm tired of being thought of as an idiot, a goon, a whacko. I'll fight when I have to, but not every game, because that's crazy. I don't have to. I don't like that image, but I'm afraid that's the image I seem to have."

Secord was a tough guy, but I wasn't surprised years later when a major airline trusted him with a plane full of people. Manson seemed genuinely dangerous, to others and primarily to himself. "When Dave Manson lost control," Jeremy Roenick said in his memoir, "he looked as if he might kill you." If a lot of guys around the league regularly assaulted opponents and the idea of civilization, you seldom felt as if they'd go berserk in the medieval sense of the word, smearing their bodies in bear fat while dropping psychotropic mushrooms. Manson, though . . . Remember how for years observers troubled by hockey violence predicted that a player would end up dead on the ice? Manson seemed as likely as anyone to be the guy standing in the police lineup while one of his teammates served the major for manslaughter. Assuming the refs called a penalty at all.

I admired Manson for the same on-ice reasons I'd admired Secord. But Secord was an uncomplicated pro. Manson passed through promise to infamy to tragedy, an irresistible story arc.

Like a lot of fiction written by young fools, my casting of Manson as Tragic Hero bore no relation to reality. In my defense, I never thought otherwise. It was practice for what I vaguely hoped would become my life's work.

Narrative helped me organize the wildly contradictory data I took in watching Manson play. Moment to moment he played like a lock-down All-Star defenseman in the making, or a second pairing mainstay with a useful mean streak, or—if you squinted— an offense-first risk-taker with a bazooka shot that made up for his defensive shortcomings. Or, well, a run-of-the-mill undisciplined blockhead.

Manson's fifty-four-point breakthrough campaign suggested the Hawks' brain trust had continued its recent streak of drafting stars, adept role players, and sundry useful spare parts. Had you told me Manson would wear a Hawks uniform in 2000, I'd have assumed he evolved into a beloved institution rather than taking a second go-round in the sweater after playing for four other teams (with Dallas and Toronto ahead of him).

It was always clear that demons tempted Manson and that the team's handling of him played a part in him giving in. But for once Bill Wirtz didn't work as an antagonist. The team already paid enough tough guys to keep the meatheads in the seats. With that part of his business plan covered, Wirtz must've seen that Manson had far greater value as an iron-nosed defenseman. His fighting only took an asset off the ice.

● Mike Keenan provided the antagonist.

Keenan fascinated, as all the magnificent villains do. To this day, I read anything about the guy, and would ghostwrite his memoir without a second thought. While I've already branded him the Manson narrative's bad guy, I never considered him evil beyond the one thin slice of his career, though I might've changed my mind if I'd played for him. I wouldn't call him evil at all, now. That's too big of a four-letter word for hockey. Also, I know more of *his* narrative.

Keenan took the Blackhawks head coaching job at a time when he reigned as The Man in the world of hockey. Having resurrected the Flyers overnight, he wore out his welcome in Philadelphia after four seasons. It amazed me and everyone I knew that the Hawks considered Keenan, let alone hired him. Superstar coaches, by definition entities unto themselves, contradicted the team's culture of Masonic insularity. To avoid the issue, the Hawks preferred to promote from within, as with Magnuson, or unearthed anonymous types like Tessier who, whatever their talents, would come into the job owing the Wirtzes a debt.

By all accounts, Keenan loved Manson. Simultaneously, he

tormented him. Sportswriters portrayed the clash as the age-old player-coach conflict, two hard-headed guys at odds. Those who ventured into the psychological warfare aspects of the relationship usually noted that Keenan only wanted Manson to live up to his potential. Personally, I had a hard time seeing how asking Manson to duke it out every other night would shape him into a star defenseman. After all, Keenan more than insisted Manson needed to play with discipline. It was as if over time Keenan became a prisoner of his own narrative: his bullying and provocations ultimately failed with Manson, and Keenan lacked the flexibility to try something else. In the meantime, Manson the budding star defenseman receded. Charlie came to the fore.

Manson seemed confused. The Verdi story vividly gets across a guy at war with what others expected of him, maybe even a guy pushed to do too much beyond his gifts. I preferred the latter for my narrative because then Manson's pain made sense. Not only did he suffer failures (physically, in his play, and mentally, in terms of discipline); he failed within a hypermasculine hockey culture that hates the very idea that anything is too much, and brands anyone who feels that way as a quitter, a pussy, or—the mortal sin in hockey—lacking commitment. Taking it further, even if Manson had chosen to play to his talents rather than to Keenan's fancies, could he have kept his job?

My narrative was so much storytelling horseshit, of course. It simplified reality, as all stories do. Less forgivably, my story was formulaic. I was too callow to recognize that Keenan had motives other than making Manson miserable, that he might really want Manson to thrive, and that, even if he didn't, he wanted to remain employed as Blackhawks coach, and was fed by a drive to succeed beyond my comprehension.

Worse, my narrative turned Manson into a tool. There's no

weaker protagonist than one robbed of agency and responsibility. That my narrative imagined Dave Manson, of all people, in that way—it was ludicrous. Hell, even Keenan antagonized Manson at his own risk. Jeremy Roenick wrote in his memoir:

> Initially, Manson took his medicine, like we all did at various times. But during Keenan's rant, Manson snapped. He stood, yanked off his shoulder pads and flung them across the locker room, just missing Keenan as he ducked out of the way. That was merely the first salvo of Manson's attack. As the pads were launched, Manson began running, in his skates, directly at Keenan. Keenan fled out the door with Manson on his tail.

Not exactly the actions of a victim.

I am embarrassed to consider how much projection went into the Manson narrative. Unrecognized genius, confusions about career and manhood, conflict with a father figure, problems with an awful temper—I should have just written it all down and handed the notebook to a psychiatrist. Still, I saw a guy in pain, and years later I'd stand by that much of my analysis.

Was it a tragedy? Well, Manson never again matched his fifty-four-point season. Once out of Chicago, he devolved into a penalty sponge and, amidst flashes of solid defensive play, a soldier signed by teams "adding a little toughness" to placate their fan base on the cheap. It sounds like tragedy to me. I'm sure he'd take full responsibility. If you've ever heard a hockey player interviewed, you can imagine his words: "Nothing to cry about. I got to play a lot of years in the National Hockey League. Mike just wanted me to be better." That's fine. Manson's version gets to be definitive. Like all of us, he deserves to create his own story.

The only notable aspect of my Manson narrative was the fact I invested so much emotion in it. Verdi's profile gratified because it backed up at least part of what I believed. I should've taken the lesson that my observations were less than singular. But I could only practice self-delusion, not recognize it.

SPRINGTIME IN ALBERTA

14

Young adulthood sands down naïveté. Maybe Keenan took on that role with his players. His wielding of belittlement, abuse, degradation, histrionics, and the rest of an extensive psy-ops toolbox replaced any notions of rah-rah team spirit with an existential reality of professionalism. The rest of us call this phenomenon *worldliness.* It's a tiresome acting out of the bumper sticker wisdom thrown at us as teens. You're nothing special. Quit feeling sorry for yourself. You'll get your ass handed to you if you fail to compete. No one ever said life was fair. You need to learn to deal with assholes. (One of my father's favorite sayings: "Son, the world is full of assholes.")

A part of me feels that Keenan-esque abuse can steer our lives in a better direction. Oh, I know better. Thanks to a mountain of academic study, we recognize such treatment does more harm than good, to the point that even the sociopathic drill sergeant of the movies exists only in fiction anymore. If I watched a coach belittling or humiliating my kid, I wouldn't thank the guy for his dedication to character building. I'd blow up his house. But the messed-up parts of my own masculinity nonetheless allow me to entertain the idea it might have helped *me.* Not my child or friends, because I wouldn't wish it on others, but me. It's laughable. Under no delusional self-appraisal do I see myself enduring that kind of treatment. I have yet to develop a thick skin, and I've never dealt with anyone remotely like Mike Keenan.

Therein lays another of the contradictions. All but the most pacifistic fathers, and not a few mothers, teach an essential lesson to boys of a very tender age: don't let other people push you around. It's foundational. When I was in kindergarten, a kid in the neighborhood bullied me when I walked home and once or twice even thumped me on the head with a book. He was much older, far into elementary school. But today I still feel a ding of embarrassment when I remember that my mother put an end to it, that I even told her in the first place. She didn't blow up the kid's house, surprising given her personality, but she did what I took even then, on some level, to be my job. If someone who can't tie his shoes yet can have a job.

Why, then, do we fans expect young men to accept treatment that, frankly, we ourselves would not (or could not) put up with? We demand that our athletes play like men, that they man up, that they be The Man. Yet fans act appalled when an athlete acts like a man and pushes back against an out-of-line boss. Any adult with agency and pride and an idea or two about boundaries might spurn the over-the-top abuse thrown at him by a middle manager who professes to make a fetish of self-control. Even the Buddha had a limit. "I refuse your gift," he once said when berated by one of his haters. Fans love to bemoan that today's millionaire players refuse to listen, but come on. A pro athlete is no longer in his teens. He has a wife and a respectable career, maybe spends a fair amount of time on charity work, and quite possibly does a pretty good job parenting a couple of children when he's not on the road. In other words, he's the mainstream, heteronormative idea of a man or at least passing. How much should we expect him to take from anyone?

• Three things run in my mother's family: fair skin, long legs, and cancer. My mom was born with the first, developed the second in her teens, and died of the third at forty-one. I mention it because Keenan arrived in Chicago the year after it happened, a season that, not coincidentally, saw me clinging to the Blackhawks. At first I dealt with the grief by turning to friends (a good idea) and drinking (a bad one). Eventually, I distanced myself from people, though also from drinking. Nights out with friends turned into quiet sessions in front of the television watching hockey. It got lonely, horribly so, but I could deal with a game. Precious little else made me feel. Placed for the first time in my life on the frontiers of intimacy with non-relatives eager to help me, I needed something to distract me when I found it impossible to connect. On off days, I immersed myself in the classes I liked and cultivated an indifference to the others that, once honed, allowed me to get an undeserved C in just about any subject at any level.

The Hawks would have killed for that grade at the time. Shaken by conflicts with Keenan and victimized by bad goaltending, the team staggered through the early weeks of the 1988–89 season. The circus trip was an especial disaster, with opposing teams putting up sixes and sevens and eights on a regular basis. On December 22, they stood at 8-22-4. The latter days of the season brought more of the same. The Hawks went into late March facing constant must-win situations and got creamed by Boston, Calgary, and Hartford, before scraping out a winner-take-all OT victory against Toronto that I watched from beneath a blanket with a walloping case of the flu. Troy Murray scored the game-winner.

It was a dull game, despite the stakes. The Blackhawks lifelessly went down 2-0. "The boos started to swell from the crowd like ominous thunder claps," the *Tribune* reported poetically. Even when the Hawks cut the lead, Toronto's Gary Leeman—set up by Ed Olczyk, no less—beat Alain Chevrier, the Blackhawks goalie with the name of the fifth Musketeer. Under normal circumstances I would have damned the Hawks and turned the channel, but *The Outlaw Josey Wales* wasn't on the Superstation, so I stuck around.

Showing savvy, the Hawks put Toronto's league-worst power play on the ice—Manson did his part, adding a last minor to his season total—and eventually tied the score.

I'd watched a lot of hockey that season, for reasons already described. I recognized the Hawks had talent. Even if I hadn't, newspapers and magazines kept telling me they did. I also remembered I had watched them slog through losing streaks without end that bookended the season and seen five different guys play goal, including Ed Belfour, a virtual unknown who despite winning an NCAA championship had gone undrafted. Really, it seemed like they suited up everyone but Alfie Moore, the minor leaguer allegedly recruited from a Toronto bar to backstop the Hawks in game one of the 1938 Finals.

The Red Wings, after a long age of mediocrity, had put aside the Dead Wings nickname we all loved and built a contender. Though ending the regular on a skid of their own, Detroit came into the series after a second consecutive first-place finish, albeit with the unimpressive 34-34-12 mark that was all it took to win the Norris Division. Like the Hawks, they brought superstar scorers and iron-willed defensemen. Like the Hawks, they employed more tough guys than a comic book mobster. Brawls had been a theme between the teams all season. The Hawks committed thirty-two penalties in the pre-Christmas matchup with Detroit. The Wings committed forty. The box score looked like the footnotes in an economics journal.

I figured the Hawks to self-destruct. Even Edmonton's return to mortality—the Oilers had sent Gretzky to Los Angeles by then—failed to ignite my usual hope that the Hawks could sneak to the mountaintop as the annual team of destiny.

Little did I realize the Hawks had reached a franchise turning point.

Let me go full-on cliché and, for the sake of narrative, say that it happened during game two. Already down 1-0 to the Wings, our heroes came out comatose, and Detroit peppered Chevrier. But amidst mayhem and endless penalty kills, Chicago took a two-goal lead, then finished the game by blowing it.

It's conventional wisdom, and therefore wrong, that this kind of late collapse means inevitable OT victory for the comeback team. Fans aren't to blame. We're fed myths about momentum our whole lives. Maybe sportswriters aren't to blame, either. They simply act as conduits for the ritual repetition of familiar words. The harm, other than the fact that believing any myth makes one stupider, is that it sows despair, leads the fainthearted and the falsely wise to turn off the game.

Exactly. The Hawks won. Duane Sutter, a man who averaged about a shot per game when he played at all, got his nightly allowance to go in.

Had the Blackhawks gone down 2-0 in the series, could they have come back on home ice? Of course. It happens all the time, just as often as the "collapsing" team rebounds to win in overtime. But, distracted by the wrongheaded wisdom of announcers and sportswriters, I wrote them off when they blew it in regulation, and with them another season. I listened to the overtime out of masochism and so I could bitch in an informed way. Their ultimate victory shamed me.

A week later, they had finished the Wings. The Blues went down in five. That left Calgary, powerhouse winners of twice as many games as the Hawks during the regular season. Even I believed when I watched them dominate the Flames in game two—

a triumph that took place in Calgary and therefore appeared on TV. We got an extra jolt of pride when the Calgary media dismissed the Hawks as worthy adversaries.

Unfortunately, game two was it for happy days. The Hawks couldn't beat the Flames' defense, though they stayed in every game despite an uncanny number of five-minute majors. The crushing moment was a game four loss in OT, after an iffy penalty called on Hawks defenseman Trent Yawney for—no kidding—closing his hand around a puck.

Calgary wrapped up the series a couple of days later. Flames coach Terry Crisp put aside his copy of *1001 Forgettable Postgame Comments* when ladling out the cold comfort quotes. "Chicago was a team bewildered and in disarray at the start of the season," he said. "Keenan and his staff has separated the wheat from the chaff and built a pretty good club, one that took us five tough games."

But a hockey fan never takes solace in the fact the better team won a playoff series. The better team loses all the time. Hell, the better team lost to the Hawks twice just that postseason.

FABLES OF A
RECONSTRUCTION

15

Between a world-class university library, a couple of newsstands, and the Sunday *Tribune* I stole from a neighbor's yard on Monday evenings— come on, clearly they didn't want it—I devoted enough study to the team to earn three credit hours.

Some of the best material came from unexpected sources. The *Village Voice*, for example, then a venerable lefty icon with fifty pages of escort ads, had a small but intelligently written sport section. Being the *Voice*, it devoted a lot of its coverage to inner-city boxers, HIV-positive marathoners, and weightlifters who injected monkey brain fluid—a lost continent of athletes and scenes—but it also covered hockey on occasion.

Its style mixed the usual analysis of NHL players and games with issues—labor problems, money, the wasp's nest of corruption just then coming to light—as yet unexplored by mags like *Inside Sports*. For instance, it was the first place I saw Paul Lukas's *Uni Watch*. The contributors also embraced hockey's absurdities. The *Voice* ran Mike Beaver's "Mixin' It Up," a review of recent fights around the league that both celebrated and satirized fisticuffs. For a time the whole of my journalistic aspirations focused on writing "Mixin' It Up" or something like it. *SI* and the *Washington Post* encouraged my ambition by reporting on the newsletter version Beaver put out in the early nineties. He perfected his jive throughout the decade, though, as shown in this fin de siècle sampling:

Dec. 1 Peter Worrell (FLA) vs. Darren Langdon (NYR) A late-fight peppering of punches by Langdon rattles Worrell's pearly whites and shows once again what everyone already knows: Langdon's got the deepest gas tank in town.

Dec. 5 Jeff Odgers (COL) vs. Rudy Poeschek (STL) Poeschek is a big-time punch thrower who gives as good as he takes when the mitts are off. Odgers is a smaller-sized version of the same. The result? They do their own version of "The Little Drummer Boy" on each other's craniums.

In the pre-internet era you had to root in thickets or join hard-to-find word-of-mouth networks to escape the mainstream coverage. Doing so, combined with dumb luck and a desperate need for escapism, revealed new angles of the sport to me. Now I wanted more than game reports, more than the edge-averse human-interest stories. Economics, power, the tension over a slow invasion by Warsaw Pact players, encroaching free agency, the dirty dealings that constituted business as usual in the NHL—those sorts of things drew me deeper and deeper into fandom. Those sorts of things, and the fact the Blackhawks started winning.

● But first the eighties had to die.
Secord retired. Bob Murray, pushed for years to hang 'em up, departed for a career as an exec. Doug Wilson remained with the team but stood on the trading block all season. Denis Savard, who had to go, went.

Keenan always feuded with his stars. Dragging down the big names, in fact, became his trademark psychological tactic. I always wondered if it mingled with his assertion of the claim to the title of the team alpha male. Keenan didn't force Savard or Wilson to dress in the Zamboni storage room, a sentence endured by Flyers center Peter Zezel when Keenan coached in Philadelphia, but it was clear he didn't want them around.

His clashes with Savard seemed as common as measurable snowfall. I idly wondered if Savvy's inveterate chain-smoking pissed off Keenan, a demon for conditioning. Of course, it was just Keenan being Keenan. New Year's Day practices. Verbal abuse. Ordering players off the ice after twelve minutes for failing to concentrate.

"I kept believing I could change him," Keenan said of Savard. "Instead, I challenged him and he challenged me in the limelight. And it was probably completely unnecessary."

Keenan assumed general manager duties. That was on June 5, 1990. Less than a month later, he traded Savard for Chris Chelios, a shocker less because the team moved one of its all-time leading scorers than because they received one of the best defensemen in the NHL in return.

The deal outraged most fans I knew. Savard had been the team's headliner for most of a decade. He hadn't turned thirty and seemed a cinch for the Hall. I liked him, too, and felt uneasy with giving up the guy described, again and again, as the one essential Blackhawk.

At the same time, one or two other people told me the Hawks had pulled off a rare steal. I was working as a gofer at a newspaper, and Dave Campbell, one of the sportswriters and an ardent Hawks fan, exclaimed, "They'll never lose again."

I was charitable enough to be happy that Savard had escaped

his nemesis. Altruism only played a part in buying into the deal, though. A few years earlier, dealing Savard would have broken my heart. But I had entered that phase of adulthood—since exacerbated by fantasy sports—where a fan starts thinking like a general manager. Savard had one more season with the Hawks before becoming a free agent. That left his representation with the unappetizing task of arguing money with General Manager Keenan. It was hard to see that deal getting done. The free agency system of the day meant the league would choose what object the Hawks received as compensation, a chilling possibility.

The season that followed made it impossible to argue with the move. With Chelios anchoring the defense and Jeremy Roenick and Ed Belfour becoming stars, and with Steve Larmer rising to near–Hall of Fame levels, the Hawks didn't join the elite; they somehow became the elite. Their style—balls-out scoring, psychotic physical play, choking defense, necessary penalty killing (they led the league in penalties), and confidence in their ability to win any battle of attrition short of the Peninsular War—ushered in an enjoyable six months.

I worked many evenings. Two things saved me. First, Sports-Channel replayed road games in the middle of the night. Second, the newspaper's poohbahs allowed a TV in the newsroom to track coverage of the first Gulf War. Let's just say the war did not last long, but the television and its cable package remained.

By January, anyone knew we had one of the great Hawks seasons of all time unfolding before us. Skating, scoring, or brawling, the players brought it, seemed capable of matching any kind of style an opponent chose to play. Every role player seemed to have the greatest season of his career. Even games that didn't count added to the blockbuster narrative. The All-Star Game at the Stadium kicked off with a jingoistically bonkers tribute to fighting the Gulf War that became the kind of Instant Memory sports leagues immediately throw into montages.

Blame the sorry end of the season on my faithlessness. I did. Having conquered the league, the Hawks lost to the mediocre North Stars in the first round. Minnesota went on to become the fabled low seed that makes the Stanley Cup Finals. The Hawks looked exhausted after playing full-out for an entire regular season. To add to the challenge, a flu epidemic swept the locker room as the postseason began.

More ominously, Keenan manifested even greater than usual extremes of behavior. At one point he gave away a power play by challenging the width of a goalie stick. He benched veterans in favor of minor league call-ups and placed goon Mike Pelsuo on his superstar line with Roenick and Steve Larmer. For whatever reason, Keenan let Doug Wilson know he was playing his last games for the Hawks. Wilson responded by taking a lacerated jaw for the team in game five and flying from the hospital to Minneapolis to beg Keenan, in vain, to play game six. It felt like Keenan's compulsion to express his message, whatever it was, had trumped his fanatical need to win.

The disastrous ultimate result eclipsed the cheap shots and off-the-play foolishness that provided loads of early series entertainment. With Manson and up-and-coming ruffian Stu Grimson matched up against the likes of boom-boom Basil McRae and the awesomely named Shane Churla, we anticipated and received a bevy of spears, the pulling of guys to the ice from behind, an eye gouge.

I pondered how I, personally, could have prevented this catastrophe. Why hadn't I sent that book of Zen koans to Keenan? What about the night I ignored the Hawks in favor of a girlfriend's come-hither look and the sound of running bathwater? It was so bad, I was too shocked to feel anger. When Keenan traded Wilson to the expansion San Jose Sharks in September of 1991, I barely noticed. Manson went to Edmonton before the season began. An era had ended, for me, too.

BETWEEN BLUE LINES
AND BORGES

16

My gofer job convinced me I wanted no future in journalism. Never mind that I'd never be able to ask grieving parents about their dead child, or that local politics wouldn't interest me unless time travel landed me in the Russian Revolution, or that my instructors assigned reading material that detailed how impending economic doom would destroy print journalism. The lifestyle, from what I could see, included too-small apartments, divorce, rootlessness, economic distress, and lower back pain. At the time that sounded unbearable. (If I only knew.)

Past my long period of depression and relieved of financial desperation, I did well in my last year of school, applying myself to a higher percentage of classes than in the past. The NHL was not so okay. Labor strife, a defining baseball narrative, had finally crossed over. Player holdouts became commonplace. Belfour stayed home when camp opened in 1991. Steve Smith, the defenseman acquired from Edmonton in the Manson deal, showed up without a contract because the Oilers refused to pay him.

The NHL wasn't exactly feudal. We had the NCAA as an example of pure athletic serfdom. But only six or seven stars received more than $1 million. The National Basketball Association, to say nothing of Major League Baseball, far outstripped that. You could see why guys might wonder why Wayne Gretzky shared a tax bracket with the third- or fourth-best pitcher on the Dodgers.

Crooked union leadership explained part of the story and added to the head-shaking reality of the NHL as a second-rate mafia. An epic of venality and ego and outright robbery, the tale of Alan Eagleson and his corrupt tenure as union chief had finally come to light. Eagleson entered hockey as Bobby Orr's agent in an era when hockey players personally negotiated their contracts and got hosed. When Eagleson screwed up negotiations with Orr's Bruins in the mid-seventies, an interlude that featured breathtaking malpractice on Eagleson's part, Bill Wirtz bailed out his Great Good Friend and took on Orr's failing knees. Eagleson managed to convince the players to let him lead the union. He then spent the eighties colluding with Wirtz, the head of the owners' group, to limit salaries and pension benefits. That was just the first line on a long list of abuses that began with taking kickbacks from insurance companies that sought to lowball injured ex-players. Did I mention that his financial malfeasance left Orr bankrupt?

An alliance of media and retired players long sick of Eagleson's chicanery broke his power and wrenched him from the Hall of Fame. This unheard-of challenge to authority and tradition planted a kick on Wirtz's well-tailored backside. His power behind the scenes, once unchallenged, slipped away. He lost the chairmanship of the Board of Governors after a five-term imperium. Worst, he lost the big chair to Bruce McNall, the coin baron and crook who brought Gretzky to L.A. after buying him from Oilers owner Peter Pocklington—himself a union-buster, felon, practitioner of fraud, and perjurer. McNall represented the kind of flash, marketing, and go-for-it fiscal recklessness at odds with Wirtz's old school vision of the NHL. That probably didn't matter as much as the fact he blew up the salary scale by paying out gobs of money.

I appreciated the chance to drop terms like *labor theory of value* into hockey conversations. Naïve about human nature despite years of Soviet history classes, I thought it especially incredible anyone would rip off Bobby Orr, let alone engage in all the other crap. The mixture of power politics and class-based perfidy tied into my studies far more than actual hockey, and I followed it as avidly as the games. The atmosphere gave me good reasons to ignore the on-ice action beyond my usual Thanksgiving start date. First, the looming strike—why get invested? Second, the hangover from the Stars collapse returned when I remembered Manson wasn't on the team anymore. Third, I'd vowed to redeem my mediocre college career with an all-out senior year effort.

Reform only went so far. Hockey became a tool, a strategy, for connecting to classmates, for (shudder) networking, and even for chat sessions with one or two instructors. Heretofore, I seldom engaged my professors, intimidated by their position and unable to believe they had any desire to talk to students. Now I could turn a polite icebreaker about what I did over the weekend into a trawl for hockey fans.

Finding another of the brethren among my peers opened doors to school-related discussions and provided companionship for barroom broadcasts. It also gave me my first experience of actively participating in a subculture beyond music—the validation, the shared secret knowledge, the oddly close friendships that can grow out of a single shared interest—and that, frankly, would have a greater effect on my life than whatever I learned in 300-level grammar.

Meeting hockey fans who were also would-be writers and working musicians and academics in the midst of celebrated careers shook one of my important assumptions as a fan. For a long time, I believed hockey and an artistic life could not co-exist. What kind of big thinker cared about sports? "Soccer is popular because stupidity is popular," Borges once declared. The statement spoke greater truths about humanity than the sport in question, but I had accepted as dogma the idea that serious minds did not waste life's precious moments on hockey.

Man, I wanted to be an intellectual snob. I resolved to leave hockey when my well-received first novel or instant-classic essay transformed me into the toast of the Manhattan hipeoisie. Granted self-confidence by the *New York Review of Books*, I'd leave such childish things behind.

In the meantime, though, showing up for class seemed like enough reform.

● In the present, a year that is long past the retirements of every-one on the 1992 team, where Mike Keenan last coached in a Rus-sian industrial city built on iron and steel—the jokes write them-selves—my phone tells me I have to empty some of my saved texts if I want to receive new ones. The 148 texts cramming the file fall into three categories: pictures of my daughter; intense conversations with a friend who went through major life changes in the past two years; and messages received during the Hawks' Cup-clincher over Tampa. Most of these texts make no sense in a vacuum. A few barely register as English. All of them are, in my tiny life, important documents. In my bluer moods, they remind me that one night in June of 2015, a lot of people were thinking of me.

JAGR IN THE HEART

17

The 1991–92 Hawks remain my favorite edition of the team. The team itself was colorful, excellent, and thrilling to watch. My own life had improved appreciably, too. The serious emotional ills had faded. I had a circle of friends, creative outlets, a regular weekly basketball game, a blond and musical girlfriend, cable, and money to buy food. Senior year, for all its anxieties, brought that liberating sense of the possible we feel when we can begin a long-awaited transition in life.

The Blackhawks added to these pleasures by taking all of the enjoyable elements of the previous season to new extremes. The spin-o-ramas and cartwheel-inducing hip checks and circus saves produced a season seemingly shot in IMAX. Everyone seemed to reach a milestone— Stu Grimson even scored a goal—while the players showed just enough color to allow fans to turn them into personalities.

Roenick overcame the immemorial law of the NHL by offering revealing quotes. Chelios and Steve Smith drew from a bottomless bag of dirty tricks seldom seen outside the recording industry. Larmer developed a public profile, his first, with a long consecutive-game streak—he never missed a game as a Hawk—and by serving in the visible job of union rep. Beyond the stars skated an agreeable assortment of scoring specialists, forechecking linebackers, vet trade-ins, muscle, a Russian (then a novelty), a five-hundred-goal-scoring Hall of Famer in his twilight years, and defenseman Keith Brown, the rarest of the rare at that time: a man with twelve years in a Hawks uniform.

Ed Belfour—mercurial in personality, fanatic in his attention to little details—pipped them all. That he held out for more money, the magic $1 million figure, no less, showed him to be one of the new breed who eschewed the typical hockey jock deference to authority. It seemed humorous at first, Belfour sticking it to Keenan the GM and Keenan the coach, until stories hinted that Belfour might get dealt to Detroit. That sounded frighteningly like the Phil Esposito fiasco.

But Belfour signed and played himself into shape while the Hawks' "popgun offense," to quote a headline, led them on a tie-laden odyssey through the 1991 part of the season. Unable to entertain one way, the Hawks did it in another, and the game misconducts rained down. Off the ice, Belfour added to his legend by turning a routine traffic stop into a visit to a suburban jail.

It was impossible to get a read on the team except that they sucked on the road. That is to say, in the games most of us could watch. The Hawks reached a nadir on January 11, an indifferently played 6-2 loss at Winnipeg. The highlight came when Keenan pulled Belfour in the second period, and Belfour flew to the bench to confront him. He's popped his cork, I thought, unsure of which person I meant, but nothing happened.

Belfour and backup Dominik Hasek—not one but two Hall of Famers—teamed with the suffocating defense to send the team on a 6-0-1 run dimmed only by injuries and the news that Roenick liked Bryan Adams enough to attend one of the Canadian singer's concerts. The playoffs began with graduation staring me in the face. Based on the previous few years, and the impenetrable mysteries of the regular season, anything seemed possible—quick elimination, a Stanley Cup, or players desperately escaping to freedom from Keenan by floating out of the Stadium on a raft of coconuts.

• Then they went on a playoff run that set records and took a chunk off my already unimpressive GPA. The Hawks hardly qualified as a surprise team, except to their more scarred, skeptical fans. The team came in third in the conference, though nothing like a strong third, a pedestrian finish Keenan blamed on Belfour's holdout.

The give-and-take early games against the Blues shaped up as another go-the-distance ordeal. Even that prediction came to seem optimistic when the Hawks gakked a 4-1 lead to lose game three in double overtime and go down two games to one. Yet they stormed back with two wins. The Blues, facing elimination at home, put shot after shot on Belfour, but only got one past him. Roenick, meanwhile, faked out a checker with a Chelios pass on his stick and scored the series winner.

I could tell people, and I did, that getting to the second round was enough. This was less cynicism than defensiveness mixed with my own lifelong willingness to settle for too little. Detroit waited, and the Wings had far more of an all-around game than the Blues. Worse, the Hawks beat them just once all season. After the Hawks took the first game, I watched the second in a campus bar, sitting at a wide table or booth "studying" with friends and beers, and expecting the Hawks to settle for a split on the road. The two loudest cheers of the night: the guy flipping the satellite TV channels landed by accident on a porn station; and Ed Belfour slugged Bob Probert in retaliation for Probert running him over in game one. The Hawks improbably swept the Wings. Seven straight wins and counting. Then came Edmonton—all the ghosts returned that spring. The Hawks demolished the Oilers

8-2 in the opening game at the Stadium (a satisfying turning of the tables), won game three in Edmonton in overtime, and finished the Oilers in four.

It was hard to argue with eleven straight victories. To graduate and enjoy a Stanley Cup win in the same year seemed a wondrous way to embark upon the post-collegiate life journey.

● One night, after binging on Billy Squier videos, I stumped YouTube's search feature with the terms "Jaromir Jagr 1992 Stanley Cup." That was long ago, before the site had matured into today's repository of all human achievement and humiliation. I knew that, when YouTube did mature, someone would post the highlights of the fateful game one, and on that day I would see if Jagr's goal played out as it ran in my memory, with him taking the puck beside the near circle and treating the Blackhawks defense like traffic cones before flipping a neat backhand past Belfour. Before the Hawks won the championship in 2010, the clip never failed to produce a physical reaction in me akin to plunging down an elevator shaft stomach first. It was the worst moment in my personal history as a sports fan.

The game one implosion against Pittsburgh was total and numbing, all the more because the Hawks, as they had in so many of that season's playoff wins, always seemed on the brink of putting the game away. Yet at the same time no lead seemed safe, not the stunning 3-0 tally, and not the 4-1 score that on the surface seemed to snuff out any chance of a Penguins surge. Wild swings from elation to gloom make for the most exhausting type of hockey consumption. Give and take is also the kind of game that demands intense attention, bad news if you plan to put together résumés during "lulls in the action."

The series offered enough cause for trepidation. Pittsburgh brought the league's most explosive offensive team. Mario

Lemieux, the best player in the world, led the way. Pittsburgh would start the final at home, and the overwhelming majority of observers favored them to repeat as champs.

To steal game one from them seemed not so much desirable as imperative, the pivot on which the series would turn. Each goal Pittsburgh scored seemed outsized, indeed, seemed gigantic. At 4-3, with five minutes left, the Hawks lived or died with whether they could run out the clock before the Pens scored again. What a hopeless feeling for a fan, to accept the inevitability of a Penguin goal as well as the certainty the Hawks would not score another. Furthermore, we could never relax because any kind of shot might go in. Lemieux had already caromed one goal off Belfour's ass.

Jagr's goal destroyed (again) all illusions that a fan, even thousands of fans, can influence a game. His goal tore out the hotline to heaven, left all prayers unanswered and turned our superstitions, the rituals of an honest pagan faith, into mere fetishism for lucky pizza toppings or whatever other damn thing we clung to as an illusory means of steering a way through an uncaring cosmos. If Jagr shook one's faith, Lemieux demolished it. In the game's final seconds, a sacred time when, by immemorial custom, referees swallowed their whistles, Lemieux coaxed a hooking call from Steve Smith, or rather from the ref. The Pens won the faceoff. Lemieux darted in alone on Belfour and won the game with thirteen seconds left.

Keenan ranted and raved after the game. Playing the refs, he charged Lemieux with diving, in between the usual trenchant criticism of his own guys.

Keenan at first served as a worthy surrogate for fans, and picked on the same targets we condemned in home and tavern. Alas, somewhere in there the man suffered an undiagnosed episode that convinced him he must use the Stanley Cup Finals to deliver another indecipherable message. In the middle period of game two, he more or less kept his top line on the bench and rolled with enforcers Peluso and Grimson "to wear [the Penguins] down a little bit." Roenick summed up the world's reaction: "He has his reasons. But I don't know what those reasons were." Pittsburgh won again.

If Keenan's behavior seemed odd until then, he soon put another wheel off the rails. Roenick, his hand bruised by an incidental slash, showed up to a press conference sporting an impressive cast. Keenan laid dark hints that not just one but two dirty Pens had deformed his star, and why weren't they facing suspension?

Theater relies on suspended disbelief, but no one bought this drama. The brazenness of Keenan's performance had a go-for-broke quality you could not credit to a stable human being. Jesus Christ, here we were, watching in agonized powerlessness, abandoned by the gods and tradition itself, a historic playoff renaissance disintegrating in front of us, and the coach of the team is spending off days masterminding stunts. Teams pay coaches to find every edge, but this didn't have the charm of, say, Keenan sneaking the Stanley Cup into the Flyers clubhouse during the 1987 final. Absconding with the Cup is a winsomely high school tactic. Should it key a comeback, the day might become hockey folklore, like finding your goalie in a bar. Keenan, though, looked flop-sweat desperate and, worse, dragged his palpably unwilling star player into the center ring of the circus.

After game three, a 1-0 loss, the team had scored all of one goal in two and a half games, and after game four, no one cared, because Pittsburgh won the Stanley Cup. By then, campus had emptied out. Among the last to leave, I watched the final game on the satellite link at a crummy frat bar, one of those stinking places you could only properly clean with fire. The game itself was fantastic, with rush after rush, crunching checks, Keenan furiously mixing and matching players, a goaltending high-wire act, and Dirk Graham, the team captain, tallying a hat trick in the first period. I lacked the present-mindedness that the Buddhists tell us orbits wisdom, or whatever they mean when they tell us to enjoy the moment. Instead I put in most of three miserable hours—the Hawks, game until the end, deserved that from me—and left rather than cry in public. I was glad to be alone, to have not made myself a fool in front of others with my disappointment, my anger, my helplessness.

The worst of it was I had put a substantial part of my brain chemistry at the mercy of ice hockey. What the hell was I doing? Starting each day by spinning a wheel marked with random moods—OPENLY WEEPING and INDIFFERENT TO ASTEROID COLLISION and CAUTIOUSLY HAPPY—would've made more sense. Astrology made less sense, slightly.

My real problem was that a substantial part of my brain chemistry was at the mercy of another force I couldn't control: my brain. The Blackhawks bore no responsibility. If anything, they had distracted me from my brain's worst depredations, had in an odd way structured the school year, to my benefit, while providing an acceptably manly obsession that proved malleable in adapting itself to various intellectual and, God knows, emotional needs.

CODA

18

The ostensible reason for Keenan's ouster from the bench was to allow the Hawks to keep their relationship with Darryl Sutter, then an up-and-comer in the coaching ranks. During this time the Hawks brass played up the interest other teams had in Darryl, and made it clear that a failure to give him a shot in Chicago meant he would take one elsewhere.

This was milieu control, of course. The situation involved power and ego and the rest of the menu alpha males order from. No one believed Keenan wanted his so-called promotion from coach-GM to full-time general manager. True enough, by November the rumors he would re-up with the Hawks for five years rose and faded. We woke up and Keenan was gone, a casualty of his own power-hungry style of management, or a victim of whatever dysfunction governed in the Hawks front office, or because he wanted to coach, or because he insisted on reporting to Wirtz, or had burned his bridge to Wirtz. As late as 2010, the story remained in dispute. Clearly, though, Keenan's understanding of psychology didn't extend to front office politics, because he never lasted very long anywhere else.

Who doubted Keenan would lose the power struggle? No one except maybe Keenan. The only surprise, and under the circumstances it wasn't much of one, was that the Hawks dumped the guy who lifted them out of a sixteen-year run split between utter irrelevancy and service as a punching bag for teams from Alberta. Dark times already loomed. Then the Wirtzes handed the team back to bumbling Bob Pulford. Hilariously described as "ubiquitous," Pulford carried all the gravitas of a substitute teacher. His return to the GM's seat announced in thundering tones that an old era had begun, one in which loyalty to the Family was paramount.

Keenan bolted for New York, won his Stanley Cup with the Rangers, and left on bad terms after one season. Sutter, meanwhile, lasted two and a half years, his tenure cut short through no fault of his own. With his dismissal the Hawks revved up machinery that pulped seven coaches in twelve years. Pulford, naturally, was one of them.

LOVE AND WINNIPEG

19

For much of the nineties, I carried a ticket stub in my wallet: Chicago versus Winnipeg at the Stadium, first balcony standing room, fifteen dollars. I attended on a first date with a woman who tolerated and maybe even liked hockey. The stub represented an experiment with sentimentality, previously something I avoided in romantic relationships because I considered it transparent. In fact, I kept the stub a secret for a long time, embarrassed by my willingness (heartfelt, true) to be corny. No fool, my girlfriend would have expected me to use the stub as a heart-melting gesture, a get-out-of-jail free card for some transgression, and I might have tried, too, had I not realized she was a lot smarter than me.

I remember very little about the game except that the Blackhawks won. With my mental energies focused on contriving ways to kiss my date, I even forgot a fight broke out within the first minute of the game, something I can remember from a dozen other occasions. Once I showed her the ticket stub, years later, it became the basis of one of those recurring jokes that bind couples. I would tease, "I bet you don't even remember who the Hawks beat," because the first time I asked she didn't. After that, she'd tease back. "Tulsa," she'd say, or "Vermont" or, most clever of all, "They lost, right? Again?"

The team's success had transformed standing room into a rugby scrum while I attended college. Once challenged to find an ideal sight line, a mob of us packed five or six deep just to see at all. The scene remained genial, though, with respect for the fandom, if not the personal space, of others. The majority of people, in truth, preferred easy access to the aisle and the stairs, to more easily load up on beer. A little patience, some polite guile, a sideways slip, and I could land a good view. I felt a pang of worry during the sudden surges forward to see a goalmouth scrum. I'd experienced that feeling at concerts, to some degree, but SRO struck like an unexpected rip tide, a force as incapable of caring as it was irresistible. Once worried about getting racked up on a railing, I now feared I'd be shot eight rows down into the balcony, with my stunned body passed around until the second intermission rush for the bathrooms emptied the seats. I never heard about injuries—I did know a woman passed around by the crowd—and wondered that they didn't happen. Then again, I found the SRO rowdies friendly and, by the second intermission, pretty blasted. Maybe the fights took place elsewhere, among people who could afford to sit and get drunk.

My date for the Winnipeg game became my girlfriend. Every year she gave me Hawks tickets for my birthday. Sometimes the two of us stood, sometimes we sat, depending on what she found available. Once she bought a single seat and an SRO ticket for a game against the Devils, and we switched off, before finally standing together.

I made less than a fortune at the job I had cadged but found a way to be young in a big city. Hockey had competition, though less for my money than my free evenings. I tried just about anything I thought capable of entertaining me or making me more cultured and, therefore, a better, more sophisticated person. I'd never stepped inside an art museum until I moved to Chicago.

Most of the live theater I'd watched before then had featured kids in broccoli costumes. Magazines at Tower Records repeatedly told me about Chicago's status as the center of the rock music universe, and I felt obligated to partake in that, since I could walk to Lounge Ax and the Vic Theater, and the Park West was right around the corner from my place.

For a while I attended any play I could afford and a few—*Miss Saigon*, for instance—I could not. There is no greater proof of my cultural illiteracy than the thought *Miss Saigon* could improve me in any way. I attended free classical music programs downtown, half-listened to presentations at the Chicago History Museum, paid cash money to watch banjoists at bars.

Hedonism led me to entertainments I enjoyed free of the burden of self-improvement. The Blackhawks plausibly, that is not to say logically, seemed to have as good a chance as ever to win it all. They were still as talented as the previous Cup team, newly seasoned, and freed from their Napoleonic scourge; you could dream they had a better chance. A rough start gave way to an indomitable December. After the Winnipeg game, I saw them trounce Gretzky and the Kings—Roenick: Zeus—before tying the sorry Nordiques and losing to Buffalo, a game I cannot remember at all despite the teams putting in ten goals.

A lot was going right in my life. In addition to a very agreeable girlfriend, I had college mates around and my coworkers were, by and large, twentysomethings too smart for their own good—funny, learned, funky, and willing to take part in the little community that sprung from the bookstore where we worked. It was like an extra year of college, except with sex and disposable income. I had an unbelievably cheap apartment in one of the city's best neighborhoods, and without a lease, as long as I agreed to vacate within thirty days of whenever the alcoholic millionaire upstairs sold the property. Even Kurt Cobain walked the earth, and the good, smart music that had emerged from the left of the radio dial to vault him to stardom had conquered all. As if to prove my generation's superior musical taste, a grasshopper swarm drove Elton John from an Australian stage the day before my birthday. Could even the Pittsburgh Penguins stand before such an alignment of omens?

Quite frankly, the Hawks provided as good a product as anyone could want. The stars played like stars, and they employed lots of them. Belfour even had Vladislav Tretiak, the Soviet Superman, coaching him. Daryl Sutter proved as competent as advertised. The rivalries of the divisional era made every game against Detroit, St. Louis, Toronto, and Minnesota an event. (Tampa Bay, not so much.) Better yet, the Hawks won many of those games. The division came down to Chicago and Detroit. The Hawks arranged to clinch over Minnesota—always satisfying, that—and Roenick scored another fiftieth goal.

The previous season cured me of undue optimism, and I had a game-seven level of anxiety working even before the puck dropped against St. Louis in the first round of the playoffs. My mood didn't endear me to my coworkers at the store, I'm sure, or to the customers, who wanted to buy *The Bridges of Madison County* and instead contended with a clerk distracted by Pat Foley's voice rising (and rising) from the boombox beneath the counter. I suppose it's amazing the store never fired me for such foolishness.

Over the next two games Chicago battered the St. Louis goaltender with shots, dazzled him with fancy moves, chipped and chopped and deflected the puck. The Hawks, not to put too fine a point on it, kicked ass up and down the ice, and nothing went in. Then nothing went in again the next game. Down 3-0 in the series, the Hawks had one player—a journeyman winger named

Brian Noonan—on the scoresheet, and he had a hat trick in the series opener. My face, and this is sadly no exaggeration, bore raw red marks from me slapping my forehead every time a sure Hawks goal turned into another Foley cry of high-tenor disbelief.

Another game four, another foregone conclusion, and I bore it stoically, my affect sane, my voice at low volume, my profanity minimal. It turned out to be quite exciting, another of the games that remind you why you endure the pain of cheering for a sports team. The Hawks, as if to take their narrative to new depths of pain, tied the game late and lost in overtime when Belfour, having left the net to play the puck, collided with a Blues player and watched the winning shot go in. Eddie destroyed his paddle against the post, a cathartic moment for all of us. The Hawks shook hands with the inferior team that had swept them and, though we didn't know it, rang out an era of winning and high expectations.

● Surrounded by literature at my retail job, I again fell under the spell of my belief that book smarts could make me a better, or at least happier, person. It was an insidious dream, of course. We all know people as miserable as they are degreed. Nonetheless I started scanning reference books on slow evenings at the store to see just what I needed to do to get into graduate school.

These kinds of half-baked plans tempted me off and on for the rest of the decade. The biggest obstacle, other than my GPA, was an inability to decide on what I wanted to study. I didn't have much interest in an academic career. Yet teaching seemed the sole employment outlet for a humanities degree, the only kind I could see myself earning. "There are lots of people with a master's in history working at Starbuck's, K. C.," a friend warned me, while in graduate school.

Sports history or, as the professors prefer to say, sport history (singular), started to gain steam in the early nineties. Relatedly, books with titles like *Cigarettes Are Sublime* made it clear that the serious study of pop culture, including sports/sport, had invaded academia. I failed to link my vague grad school plan to a dream of leading a seminar on, say, hockey in film, or the ethnomusicological implications of screaming during the National Anthem. Had that flash of imagination come to me, standing there at the till, wondering what to do with my life, I might have found my destiny as a hockey historian.

This particular strand of disappointment in myself didn't occur to me for almost twenty years, when I went to do research at the D. K. (Doc) Seaman Hockey Resource Centre in Toronto. Located on the edge of the city, the Centre stores the relics that cannot fit in the Hockey Hall of Fame while also warehousing items donated by the public. Archiving and authenticating those items is the job for the staff. I only wish that in 1994 I had been aware that this was the kind of dream job that would have landed me on a special edition of *Oprah*.

From what I could tell, this was the typical day's to-do list: cataloging a pile of gloves and sticks; taking down details from donated jerseys from all levels of hockey; and finding a place for then-rookie Bill Gadsby's 1946 Chicago Blackhawks team jacket. Everything from gloves and skates to paintings and board games comes through the door, with a fair amount of it arriving without so much as a return address. Miragh, the very patient staffer who helped me out, told me one of her colleagues had just received a call from a security guard in Chicago who had found his grandfather's gear from c. 1905 and thought the Centre might be interested.

These people work in the world's greatest office space. Magnet schedules of all descriptions wallpapered the filing cabinets. A Camrose Kodiaks game puck sat on the file extinguisher. Atop one cabinet, amidst mugs and a Mr. Potato Head in a Blues jersey and hockey-themed commemorative bottles of maple syrup, stood a Wayne Gretzky Golden Honey Shreddies cereal box. An army of bobbleheads, with Maple Leafs star Mats Sundin a dead ringer for Yul Brynner in *Westworld*, stood at attention.

The door to the archive itself opens near a long rack of used sticks from all eras sorted by player. The collection includes one of Stan Mikita's extreme banana blades, the stick that changed hockey. As a rule, staffers wrap gear and many other items in clear plastic. Nothing that comes in gets washed.

The Centre keeps the actual Hart, Vezina, and other trophies when the hardware is not making an appearance elsewhere. Pucks never mingle with trophies, because when a rubber puck degrades it releases sulfur that harms the metal. One corner holds stacks and stacks of canned film, not far from lights scavenged from the old Maple Leaf Gardens. There's also a cardboard cutout of a Soviet player selling deodorant. And the beer Barack Obama lost to Canadian Prime Minister Stephen Harper by reasonably betting on Roberto Luongo to choke in the 2010 Olympic final.

To say nothing of the team cardigans worn by players in earlier eras. Nothing says old time hockey like a cardigan. I know players in the forties were paid in puppies, but a sharp cardigan sounds like a nice perk. There's even hockey art, in the form of Andy Warhol's portrait of New York Rangers star Rod Gilbert.

Thus, the mouthpiece that Patrick Kane tossed into the air after scoring the winning goal in the 2010 final now belongs to history. No one knows what happened to the puck, but someone had enough sense to mail in the mouthpiece. A suds man like

Kane no doubt appreciates its placement beneath a commemorative Old Style can.

In time I became a faux historian, writing library books on bubonic plague and other catastrophes for kids. No one ever contracted with me to write a hockey book, proof positive that the free market fails to use intellectual resources in a fully wise way.

ALL LOCKED OUT

20

Superstition held me for years. I was a slave to odd little habits—putting shoes on in this order, and the like. It grew out of uncontrolled anxiety, as my disordered mind attempted to game the randomness of the world in my favor. I took to believing the worst would happen in the hope that such an attitude would head off real misfortune, as if higher powers would look down and, seeing me good and scared, give me a break. That belief declined as I traded childhood Catholicism for belief in a cruel and indifferent universe. It took maturity and medication to put the final end to superstition. I know this from hockey. During the 2010 and especially the 2013 playoffs, I kept up so many tics I could barely remember to do them all. Prescribed drugs, on the other hand, let me watch the 2015 postseason with total freedom of movement and relative peace of mind.

Not so in the mid-nineties, though. I would sit on my girlfriend's floor in a pose that looked like the Spanish Inquisition's interpretation of yoga. "You're afraid to move, aren't you?" she would ask. When I finally did—after the Hawks fell behind by five goals, say—she'd laugh as I tried to stand. If the Hawks scored while I drank Rolling Rock at a bar, it was Rolling Rock until the final horn, who cared if it tasted like carbonated paste? "There's a stool open, you know," a friend might say as the Hawks led 3-2. "Why don't you sit down?" "Maybe in forty-four minutes, twenty-one seconds," I'd answer.

I was spending great amounts of mental energy on this nonsense even as I reached what the meteorologists of men's souls refer to as the Mature Stage of sports fandom. Everyone passes through that phase in his or her own way. My journey just amplified my earlier behaviors. More games. More jerseys. More beer. More angst. Twice I chose hockey—or, worse, worry over hockey—over romantic intimacy. Mind you, on both occasions I knew the union of flesh and soul with my one and only was more important and infinitely more enjoyable than a road game at Calgary that took place in the middle of an eight-game losing streak during a lockout-shortened season. But I couldn't let go. My God, it was Calgary. Who cared?

"You're becoming obsessed," my girlfriend told me, a little taken back. I think I had just finished a think-out-loud monologue on the state of the team, the Hawks, I mean, not she and I. Really, though, the Blackhawks were less an obsession than an eccentricity, one I admit I cultivated. Being identified as a cultish Hawks fan helped me stand apart, like the jeans tucked into my paratrooper boots. See, I wanted so badly to become bohemian as well as intellectual. Without seeming bohemian, you dig, because bohemians aren't manly. Also, I wanted my own quirks, rather than the clove cigarettes and world-weary irony and other clichéd signifiers indulged by my trying-too-hard peers.

Too neurotic for free love and too eager-to-please to cultivate true nonconformity, I ended up a dismal failure as a hipster. Hockey, a meathead and un-punk-rock enthusiasm, was just one more mark against that excluded me from the lives of the dancing, smoking, and cooler-than-anything young women I had desired since puberty. Eccentric remained my ceiling. Eccentric can be cute, even charming. But it is never sexy. That's why we apply the word to old men.

My girlfriend's analysis aside, true obsessiveness eluded me. I could never go into credit card debt for season tickets or put aside caring about the scorn of hockey-indifferent women. Self-awareness, as usual, defeated me. The Hawks had, like writing, evolved into a way of avoiding myself. It might have worked, had the winning team of the early nineties not turned into a disaster.

● Mind you, the Blackhawks faced a trough no matter what they did. Though huge amounts of talent from Russia and its former allies entered the league, the Hawks had no chance at any of the newcomers, because Keenan-era success had handed them a series of low draft picks. Wheeling and dealing left the team without a first-rounder in 1996 though by then they had scored the sometimes useful Sergei Krivokrasov and—in the fourth round, no less—Éric Dazé, a near-star with a great shot and a lousy back.

Sometimes useful described many Blackhawks players in those days. On nights when several were useful, they won. For a while you could fool yourself that they had enough to go on a postseason winning streak. By the end of the mid-nineties, they ceased providing even that longshot hope. *Sometimes useful* trended toward *rarely useful* and then *definitely considering being useful, will get back to you.*

Sports-related descents into ineptitude serve as a years-long reminder that plutocrats exploit our passion and their hired stooges piss it away. The Hawks, though, attacked the basic problem of building a team with a combination of cynicism and outright anger that, to be honest, was shocking even for longtime observers.

Budding free agency, and the usual escalation in salaries that follows, destroyed the illusion that the Chicago Blackhawks were a family. Team owners across sports love that metaphor, of course, and hockey poohbahs most of all. The league had cultivated the idea since Eddie Shore—a violent, ruthless, frequently out-of-control older brother—roamed the rinks, and it had become dogma defended by the alliance of owners, old-time sportswriters, and lifelong season-ticket holders. Family fit in with hockey's image of itself as a game of *real* people—red of blood, white of skin, and blue of collar—who valued hard work and loyalty as virtues on a par with faith and patriotism. Going into the nineties, hockey had largely avoided the things sportswriters loved to complain about. No huge drug scandals. No mouthy, dark-skinned college boys with chips on their frighteningly sculpted shoulders. No power-hitting millionaires demanding ever more money. No institutionalized cheating (that we knew about). No relocating teams in the middle of the night. Criticism of hockey mostly focused on fighting and a few crooked owners, both things as old as the league itself.

The Wirtzes belabored Family, Loyalty, and Hard Work to a degree that was excessive even within the sport. Let's be fair: they practiced, to some degree, what they (endlessly) preached. The Hawks maintained an alumni network that ex-players enjoyed, the team remained proud of its past heroes—Bobby Hull excepted—and the Wirtzes had by all accounts helped out Blackhawks both current and former in a variety of ways. It complicated the average fan's relationship with Dollar Bill to hear him praised by his players, and to see those players not just buy into the myth but live it through charity work that, individual good deeds aside, hung halos on the owners of the franchise.

Free agency, and the labor battles it unleashed, ushered in a new age. Furthermore, it showed that not nearly all of the players had believed the myth in the first place. A friend lamented that hockey was becoming baseball, a sport he hated almost as much as he hated the idea of labor unions. Family, Loyalty, and Hard Work, meanwhile, became a weapon to use against ingrates. This mirrored the behavior in lots of real families.

The Wirtzes wielded power well. Hawks fandom split into camps. Traditionalists who wanted to keep the old ways sided with Bill. Soulless mercenaries who preferred to win—my hand is up—knew the family sold enough booze to shower Jeremy Roenick with the wealth of a pasha. The vast, mushy middle wanted both, somehow, as the mushy middle does, an outcome only possible if the players ignored their own value. America On-line had its Hawks board, and I liked to dial in on my screeching 28.8 modem to check up on the community's anger. A majority of the posts riffed on the greed and disloyalty of players, an attitude also reflected in letters to the editor. The Tower Records down the street carried out-of-town papers, and the Toronto *Star* was a great source for this sort of thing.

Steve Larmer left first. Depending on the story, he jumped to New York either due to a salary dispute with the Wirtzes or because he saw the Hawks careening toward a cliff. I remained innocent enough to think Roenick wouldn't follow, because I bought in when he said how much he wanted to retire a Black-hawk, and because I couldn't believe the Hawks would ditch someone a good number of people saw as a budding Hall of Famer. As early as 1993, Roenick had told the papers he had to think about the future. To that end, he put his house on the market. At the same time, the ROENICK A HAWK FOR LIFE? headlines shoveled the false hope.

"He's going to be with us, is all, the way Stan Mikita was with the Chicago organization his whole career," added Shovelin' Bob Pulford. "He's a great player like Denis Savard and Mikita were for the club."

Roenick obviously saw through the charade, the same charade

perfected by hockey team execs decades before his birth. A lockout happened, and he had his knee blown out against Dallas, and for the better part of eighteen months the B.S. and threats flew in equal amounts. As Roenick neared free agency in the summer of 1996, a buddy and I hashed out the situation. With the clarity that only alcohol can give, we jumped through the open door to conspiracy theories—the real national sport of the 1990s—and speculated that the team wanted an excuse to tank and just rake in the dough at the brand-new United Center. We also agreed Wirtz had abandoned hockey for his real estate and liquor distribution in a fit of pique over the advent of free agency, and wondered if maybe the old man drank too much, though we knew he'd suffered a stroke and couldn't drink.

"I'm sick of the Hawks' crap," Main Man said. I had no idea what crap he referred to, since the Hawks had consistently won since 1988, but I'm sure I made an affirmative noise into my beer glass.

"The only thing the guy understands," he went on, "is money. We have to hurt Wirtz economically."

"Right," I said.

"We know how he makes his millions—real estate and liquor. We don't rent from him. We don't drink his booze."

"We should quit drinking to punish Bill Wirtz?" I asked.

It took him a week or so to let go of the idea.

"We have to give up booze," he said another time. "While there's time."

I asked what he meant.

"Because you know if they trade him we'll drink even more and make Wirtz richer," he said.

In the end, though, both of us held to the noble and boneheaded belief that a real fan supports the team come what may. So we stuck when the Blackhawks, after weeks of acrimony and rumor, traded Roenick. They got back a minor leaguer, a pick, and the doomed Boris Zhamnov, a merely good Russian player in an era when everyone else seemed to have a superstar from that tortured, chilly nation. Though the Roenick deal offered none of the false hope that follows a big trade, Hawks management hyped the deal. "There are not many centers that have the skill that Zhamnov does," coach Craig Hartsburg told us, without adding, "Roenick being one of them and then some."

The inevitability of change discomfited me even in the micro, I suppose because it reminded me that everything in this life is uncertain. Change also meant others moved on while I felt I didn't. Such thoughts always made me dissatisfied with myself. With the Blackhawks, I never took their success for granted. I watched the games, read the stories, recognized that the same cycle then reducing the once-unstoppable Oilers to also-rans would soon grind up my team. Yet an inability to appreciate what I had affected every other area of my life. That trait, or flaw if you prefer, harmed me over and over. Hockey, for once, had a valuable lesson to teach me, and I had no idea.

BIG IN JAPAN

21

The Hawks seemed weary not only of rising salaries but the kind of personalities the league wanted to promote in its quest to copy the NBA's conquest of the zeitgeist. Ed Belfour took his half-written Hall of Fame plaque to Dallas, after the Hawks sentenced him to the usual half-season of hard labor in San Jose. Belfour didn't fit with Chicago. No man offering pungent opinions with unfiltered, brooding resentment could hope to do so. If he lacked Roenick's heart-on-the-sleeve charm, he also seemed incapable of insincerity. A smarter league interested might have shaped Eddie into a mulleted Heathcliff, dour and obsessive, incapable of forgetting a wrong. You may not want those traits in your spouse, but in a star athlete it can make for damn fine drama.

Except the NHL hated drama. It hated interesting. The league expressed, time and again, its desire to follow the NBA's template. It hired an NBA exec as commissioner. Yet the NHL couldn't overcome the culture lag that, in many ways, rooted the league in the 1950s, and, worse, the old fantasy 1950s of Brylcreemed good citizens that it had peddled for ages. The NBA grabbed a generation with a great on-court product and charismatic athletes, true, but also thanks to an affinity for extracurricular soap opera that awed the writing room for World Championship Wrestling. The NHL, by contrast, wanted you to respect its values, or, rather, the values it upheld in the fantasy version of itself. Its real values—selling every tradition to the highest bidder and letting carpetbaggers shift teams to places like Dallas, the least-loved city in the United States—did not poll so well. You got the message that the NHL couldn't even sell out effectively.

I may have taken the state of the game too personally to make an accurate appraisal. I evangelized for hockey. I wanted a bandwagon fit to burst, an apotheosis for the sport. Let the NHL match the NBA in cred, in popularity, in drama-driven madness. If the glowing puck that Fox Sports used in its broadcasts trained a new and gigantic generation of fans to watch hockey games, great, I was on board. In fact, I often watched parts of Fox games no matter who played out of a vague impulse to support the league.

When the NHL announced that it would let its players participate in the 1998 Olympics in Japan, I was as sure as Gary Bettman that the event would seduce a generation of sports fans into hockey cultdom. Some of the best American players ever committed to wear the red, white, and blue uni. Their determined faces filled ads across media while sportswriters, a few of them paid to understand hockey, hyped the unprecedented American prowess. The public, primed for two weeks of winter jingoism, boned up on names and uniform numbers, while NBC pumped up the threat of the Swedes and Russians in order to lay pavement for a new miracle.

Bombed by Canada and Sweden, the U.S. men advanced out of the group stage only after beating Belarus at an arena called The Big Hat. Then the Czechs, like everyone else, scored four goals against the Americans. That was that. Some U.S. players stayed in the news by trashing a room or two in the Olympic Village. Broken chairs and misadventure-by-fire extinguisher, mild rock star misbehavior in other contexts, became The Shame of

America. "Next time, just stay home," Ken Rosenthal said in his column. As the Czechs rolled on to the gold, the outrage piled higher and higher. Crazy threats flew like pucks. The IOC threatened to ban American players. The NHL's commissioner promised blood. A Japanese housekeeping contractor angrily rented a carpet cleaner. A friend of mine ranted and raved about how they had made the country look bad. I wanted nothing of it, and we parted on his muttered words that I needed to expect more of our athletes. What could I say? I myself had destroyed furniture out of frustration. I once threw a bike into a swimming pool. It was hockey. These men punched each other for a living. Japan got off easy.

Blackhawks players held center stage throughout the scandal. Chris Chelios, captain of Team USA, took up the challenge of explaining what had happened. Three other Hawks (Tony Amonte, Keith Carney, and Gary Suter), plus Roenick, staffed the team's ranks, and like everyone else they fell under suspicion. Chelios penned an apology on behalf of his teammates and paid for the cleanup. Bill Wirtz also appeared in a flash of fire and aftershave to weigh in, and in surprisingly literary fashion.

"It seems like all you gentlemen are great fans of Jonathan Swift in that you use exaggeration for effect—like the Brobdingnagians and Lilliputians in *Gulliver's Travels*," Wirtz said. For good measure, he mocked the league office as out of its depth and also paranoid—Captain Queeg was mentioned—and, in a mawkish postscript that could only emerge in an NHL context, declared he would be proud to have any player on Team USA as a son.

● It says something about the Blackhawks that *Sudden Death*, a Jean-Claude Van Damme vehicle, provided one of my favorite hockey-related memories of that time. Sure, I went into the theater stoked. Hollywood had re-discovered hockey. What truer sign of the game's impending mass market breakthrough?

The film's plot came from the wife of Pittsburgh Penguins then-owner Howard Baldwin, one day to produce *Mystery, Alaska* not long after leading the Pens into bankruptcy. Van Damme plays a fireman haunted by a terrible mistake. Powers Boothe was the heavy, while NHL scoring machine/soldier of fortune Luc Robitaille, playing the Penguins' star player, uses the F-word in French.

Van Damme's character possesses a skill set that runs from installing infant car seats to martial arts prowess. He starts the fun by overcoming a terrorist—disguised as the Penguins mascot—with a washing machine. Boothe, meanwhile, threatens to kill the U.S. vice president. Since no one would care if that happened, he adds what we in the writing business call dramatic tension by holding Van Damme's daughter hostage and rigging a hockey stadium to explode at the end of a decisive Stanley Cup contest between the Penguins and Blackhawks.

I saw *Sudden Death* at the Brew 'n View at the Vic, a Chicago institution that in those days allowed you to watch movies while smoking and drinking Leinenkugel Red. The audience immediately gave up on the Van Damme portion of the movie and treated the hockey game like the real thing. Cheers erupted whenever the faux Hawks scored. Boos and profanity answered the Penguin tallies. When "Ed Belfour" let in a soft one, some guy even moaned, "Come on, Eddie." You missed nothing, that was the great thing. Van Damme suffered a setback whenever Chicago scored and kicked butt around Pittsburgh goals.

Given the film's pedigree, you had to figure the Hawks would lose. Sure enough, Van Damme spends part of the third period disguised as Pittsburgh's goalie and the Hawks still can't score, even though we had the "Let's go, Hawks" chant going.

Robitaille tied the game on a last-second breakaway. Personally, I could forgive him for denying the Hawks a pretend Stanley Cup. It was much worse that his movie heroics led to overtime and sentenced a hundred people to twenty more minutes of *Sudden Death*. But watching the Hollywood version was far more enjoyable than the 1992 Finals and, increasingly, the product trotted out for us in real life.

ONWARD AND DOWNWARD

22

You can find pleasure supporting a bad hockey club. Tickets are easier to get, and you rejoin the cult of those In The Know, in possession of the great secret that is your crummy team. Your very presence in the seats or on the couch proves you capable of loyalty, a great virtue. As the bandwagoners flee to seek out new scenes, you no longer have to share the team with frat boys or fat cats or whatever other demographic groups you despise.

In these circumstances the players, more than ever, became your boys. You appreciate the little things again—the line change made with martial efficiency, the competent forecheck, a blue-liner's crisp pass out of the zone. It's just unfortunate these things happen only once or twice per game. On a good team, a guy like Zhamnov or Amonte or Éric Dazé—the Hawks' offensive stars of the era—will get overlooked. On a mediocre team, our appreciation of them is sincere. At the same time, admiring the non-stars becomes condescending, like being proud of the worst kid on your son's Little League team when he manages to throw the ball forward. An honest affection develops. If the player meets reduced expectations enough times, and if he doesn't otherwise insult the hometown fans with obvious disloyalty or apathy, fans might see him as a victim of fate, i.e., ownership. Otherwise, he's just a journeyman. All you can hope for is a flash here and there, and good value for him at the trade deadline.

The decade played out as a descent into averageness, then desperation, and finally cynicism.

In 1996, I could still watch the Hawks beat a loaded Colorado team on Leap Day. Roenick centered the tying goal for Amonte, Chelios and his college running buddy Gary Suter prowled the blue line, Belfour watched from the sidelines with a bad back, and Dazé had yet to start suffering from *his* bad back. The U.C. was packed, and Hawks coach Craig Hartsburg seemed competent. Six months later, Roenick had left for Phoenix to start his odd post-Chicago career as a gun-for-hire who ricocheted from troubled son to Hall of Fame talent to injured vet while suiting up for four teams (and Phoenix twice). Belfour, in his new Stars uniform, shut out the Hawks while the crowd chanted, "Eddie, Eddie." Steve Smith had retired. Chelios eventually made his exit for Detroit amidst public charges of disloyalty, that worst of slurs, the one the Wirtzes sometimes turned to when asked to spend money they didn't want to spend.

Meanwhile, Zhamnov turned out to be seventy cents on Roenick's dollar. Amonte added a very long chapter to his hard-luck career by serving as the franchise face during ownership's seasons-long tantrum against changing ways.

It got worse.

● In the fall of 1998, I had a publishing job that gave me non-dial-up, reliable internet access for the first time. Since no one could reach me through my lousy hookup at home, I would get to work and find messages about the disgrace the Hawks brought to hockey. This litany of anger—some of it from friends, some from people I had never met but who were CC'd on messages from friends, some message board acquaintances—started in preseason. That was all the proof I needed that something special was in the works. Forgoing my usual slow slide into the NHL season, I tuned in for the last one or two preseason tilts. Management's strategy became clear. Unable or unwilling to build an actual hockey team, the Blackhawks intended to fill seats by the wholehearted embrace of tough-guyism.

"They're assholes, K. C.," one friend told me, both in email and in person, a typical charge. His Wings had moved away, a bit, from brawling, as speedy play by Russians and Swedes propelled them to the top of the league. Even the star players found misadventure. Gary Suter ended the season of Anaheim star Paul Kariya, at the time expected to help Canada win the gold medal in the upcoming Olympics. The commissioner gave Suter four games. The league gave him two bodyguards after he received death threats.

EXCEPT IT ACTUALLY HURTS

23

On the way up, Detroit jettisoned Bob Probert, their efforts to alleviate his substance-abuse and legal problems a failure. Probert, after suspensions and arrest-related inactivity, landed with the Hawks. It was a classic narrative arc: scare me, then be my friend. A sad number of Hawks fans fell for it.

In an uncertain fiscal age, tough guys offered good value. Most earned at the low end of the league wage scale while serving as one of the locker room stalwarts. Fans always knew a tough guy's name, and a great many of them showed up hoping for a glimpse of their man in action.

Look, I wasn't above it. Over the years I had cheered myself hoarse during bloodbaths with St. Louis or Minnesota, felt a surge of adrenalin when an opponent got his in the corner, roared when Opponent X went head over heels into the bench. The temporary insanity caused by sports violence makes a shambles of any worldview promulgated by mere philosophy or faith. On the one hand, sports provides an acceptable forum for expressing the rage, frustration, envy, and other negative emotions we swallow in everyday life. On the other, it unleashes the ugly tribalism that any team nurtures to guarantee for repeat business, a tribalism based in rage far more than in dubious but oft-mentioned virtues like civic pride.

We will accept criticism of our clothes, our work on the Turner account, or our relationship with the cat, yet five words of shit talk about The Team transforms us into an apprentice soccer thug. I once got in an argument, a real red-faced argument, over Hawks defenseman Bryan Marchment. Decided: whether Marchment deserved the epithet "goon." These days the people who remember Marchment recall a well-traveled bruiser suspended a dozen times or more, often for trying to injure other players.

I have no idea how I defended my stance. Marchment had no relationship to Chicago beyond his work uniform. The Hawks didn't draft him; they traded for him. He was Canadian, not local. The team employed him for maybe sixteen months, total. Finally, he hurt guys on purpose, abhorrent behavior even in the NHL's culture.

The why is self-evident: tribalism. In calm moments, like the off-season, I mourn—I mean, feel genuine regret—that I buy into a system that whips up tribal loyalties on purpose, for money, that pits human beings against each other, before feeling even dirtier because I suspect that's the reason professional sports exist in the first place.

Probert was no Marchment. He stalked the ice as the hands-down, fists-up star tough guy at a time when goons gave up their former jobs as policeman and bodyguards to become the brand names in a sideshow. To have Bob Probert join your team in that era—well, let's just say the man once derided as "Cementhead" became forever "Probie" to Chicago fans. It was grotesque but understandable in the context of human nature. Also, at the time, we didn't have much else to love.

The Blackhawks, and by proxy every team employing a guy willing to drop the gloves with Probert, earned off his old outlaw image. Probert received an indefinite suspension after the legendary cocaine-in-his-pants incident of 1989. A certain kind of fan considered him hockey's answer to Keith Richards, perhaps the only truly *cool* player in a league that prided itself on stoicism and hidebound conservatism ("tradition") and pandered hard to a kind of self-identified blue collar fan that admired such traits.

Like Keith Richards, Probert had moments that were outrageous to the point of disbelief. In Detroit, he lived within walking distance of the stadium because the State of Michigan declined to let him drive. He punched a goalie in the face even though the goalie was wearing his mask. He slugged fellow tough guy Craig Coxe so many times he let the refs stop the fight because he was too tired to swing anymore. Another time he fought with one hand while rehabbing a rotator cuff injury. Overlook that he was destroying himself—and we didn't even know what all those counter-punches were doing to his brain—and you had to laugh at the sheer lunacy. I certainly did.

Probert's arrival felt inevitable. The Hawks deeply believed in the NHL canard that you need only get tougher to get better. They did get him clean or cleanish, depending on whom you ask. He seemed happy. Are you kidding? After getting to Chicago he smiled all the time. It was the weirdest thing. And even in decline, when he had traded the old animalistic fury for a solid professionalism, he obviously enjoyed his work. In an era when stars defected from the Blackhawks and kept defecting, Probert's notoriety sold.

You can see why management asked: Hey, why not double down on the goon stuff? What? It's cheaper? Definitely double down.

They got Dave Manson's agent on the phone and brought back a shadow of the Keenan-era player. A bunch of other rough-and-ready meatheads (Reid Simpson, Doug Zmolek) filled the roster around him. Early on in the season we started hearing about a minor-league tough named Dennis Bonvie, a guy with a 522-penalty minute season on his resume. Why kind of mutant could this be? The Hawks pointedly dressed Bonvie in number 44, not long before the number of slugger Mike Peluso. Bonvie suited up for a St. Louis game and got thumped by Tony Twist, one of the biggest names in the NHL fight club. It was a deflatingly one-sided punch-out, with the hated Twist demolishing the illusion the Blackhawks could at least win the brawls, and the moral victories thereby.

The Hawks burned through a head coach (former team captain Dirk Graham) who never head coached an NHL team again and replaced him with another head coach who never coached an NHL team again. Chelios spent the season not on the trading block until the Hawks traded him. On March 1 came the incredible sentence: "The loss dropped the Hawks to 17-37-8, the first time in 42 years the Blackhawks have been 20 games under .500."

Wise businessmen, the Hawks brain trust didn't put all their bets on pimping violence. They also paid superstars Doug Gilmour and Paul Coffey to suit up. Both arrived in town in their mid-thirties and long past their primes. Both had bad backs. You only hire guys like that to sell jerseys and gull the rubes. The former worked for sure—I could always look down from the balcony and see red Gilmour sweaters. The Hawks even brought in hometown boy Ed Olczyk to rope in the sentimental types and then promptly sent him to the minors. Coffey, meanwhile, put in all of ten games for the team.

It was tough to watch but not nearly as tough as learning that ownership really did take all of us for morons.

● Talk about a time of transitions. I moved to a new job. It was minor league, compared to where I started, but I made more money and had manager in my title. My Lincoln Park studio with the low, unchanging rent went under the wrecking ball and I ended up in a one bedroom. My long-term relationship needed to end. It suffered from many problems, none of them original, but mutual indifference was the worst. Neither of us knew how to call it quits, though, and the shared unhappiness that dragged on through those two years led to dissatisfaction with other areas of our lives. I can't speak for her. But I found my new career boring. Many of my best friends had moved away. Turning thirty scotched my youthful dreams. I longed for the totems of legitimacy yet had no idea how to seize them. To cope with these and other messes, I wandered into a thicket of bad habits—drinking too much, romantic betrayals, ignoring significant health problems—and by the time the Hawks turned to pure crud, my misadventures began to take a toll.

Maybe I had too much conflict in my own life to enjoy hockey fights as entertainment. Maybe aging and the domesticating influence of women mellowed me out. Maybe I realized those blows to the chops actually hurt the players.

My own conflicted feelings aside, the Hawks ruined the idea of fighting. Not because they were bad at it. Beyond Probert they employed plenty of capable operators. But they made a joke of it. Whatever your thoughts on fighting in the game, the Hawks mocked the idea that tough guys played a necessary role. In so doing they mocked tradition itself.

If tribal feeling puts a part of our self in the Hawks jersey, a beatdown by Tony Twist wounded my sense of self as a Blackhawks fan and as whatever illusory self I saw reflected in the virtues of the guys on "my" team. Yet even Twist, a man employed solely to fight other men, recognized what was happening as nonsense. He hooked up with Bonvie again later in the season and seemed insulted he had to slum. I could dislike Twist as an opponent, but not when he had to drop 'em with a bop bag like Dennis Bonvie. Twist at least belonged in the league.

Dramatic features on players, Olympics coverage, glowing pucks, Sunday games of the week—all had failed to raise the NHL's profile or, for that matter, make its ratings competitive with NASCAR. Faced with the undeniable calculus of failure, Bill Wirtz chose goonery as his Cemetery Ridge, just another among many of the bad decisions made by him and his men.

The violence went beyond the fights, though. You could say "it's an emotional game" all you wanted, but the escalation in fighting seemed to give players greater sanction for intent-to-injure plays. Colorado Avalanche winger Claude Lemieux, a skilled-enough guy who for whatever reason chose to be the consensus dirtiest player ever, almost killed Kris Draper of the Red Wings by checking Draper from behind, into the bench. It's an emotional game.

That Draper's teammate Darren McCarty beat Lemieux to a pulp the next spring—the Zamboni failed to cover up the blood, and that's not a joke—made it seem like justice served. But surgeons had to rebuild Draper's jaw and face and put his teeth back in place. He missed months of hockey and, for that matter, of eating without a straw. He suffered a concussion. That's a couple of serious injuries and *no one on earth believed that Lemieux did it by accident.* Getting beat up by Darren McCarty didn't seem quite equitable, especially when it came out later that McCarty's first punch knocked Lemieux unconscious.

It's an emotional game. These kinds of things always happened. Tradition.

Pro athletes need aggression, whether they play hockey or soccer or chess. Without it, you ain't no pro athlete no more. But the NHL's atmosphere encouraged frankly insane manifestations of anger. Jeremy Roenick, playing for Phoenix, slashed Tony Amonte in the face because of a mid-game fight with his wife. And Amonte had been his close friend since high school. That kind of thing just didn't happen in other sports.

No data exists on how often a player's personal life led to violence on the ice, not for 1999 and not for 1955. For all I know Lemieux argued with his accountant that night in Denver. But did Draper or Amonte deserve to get his face rearranged because the emotional game happened to get emotional for the wrong reason?

I didn't know the inside culture of the game. I did know anger often escalated into what human resources manuals call inappropriate workplace behavior. Maybe they'd use the term *dangerous behavior* if the rest of us worked in an emotional business. Anger costs people their jobs every day, outside of hockey. It costs them money and friendship. It costs them the most important things in their lives. Even if hockey violence stirred up the testosterone—there's no doubt it did with me and thousands, millions, of other fans—I had reached a point where I could've lived with a game that eschewed serious injury, even to Claude Lemieux, in order to keep me entertained. Cheering on young men to—let's be honest—hurt each other had made me uneasy in the past. Now I felt guilty and responsible.

My era of peak fandom ended with a meaningless 2001 matchup versus the Blues. A friend and I walked up and bought tickets to the tier with the wait staff, a forty-dollar ticket then. The game offered little promise. San Jose had just destroyed a listless Hawks team. St. Louis led the league in points. The team had baffled its fan base by handing Steve Sullivan—a man waived just sixteen months earlier—a breathtaking three million per season, tied for highest salary on the team.

We settled back for easy-access beers. The Hawks racked up six goals and played so well that suspense went by the boards early on. It was a big, noisy crowd, the size and level of inebriation helped by the unusual Friday night start. Sans context you could imagine the Blackhawks ran out a competitive team deserving of rock solid support. With context, you realized it was one of those inter-divisional tussles that liven up February games in hopeless seasons, with victory midwifed by the many St. Louis stars then sitting on the injury list.

Enough beer eclipses context. Each of us also had enough going on in real life to reduce hockey to an enjoyable distraction. My friend had of late begun a new job in Chicago. I had become involved with my future wife and had a one-way plane ticket to Europe. Usually I fled from life to the Blackhawks because I could always make hockey comprehensible. That night, I escaped the Hawks to embrace a reality that promised more than they did.

LETTING GO, TAKING ON

24

The trouble with skimming a Blackhawks era as dreadful as the early aughts—the trouble in story terms, I mean—is that you hamstring the old reliable redemption narrative. It is also dishonest, I suppose, and an admission that the team's irredeemable awfulness transformed me into a fairweather fan.

Whether due to infirmary or disinterest or pique or incompetence, Dollar Bill and his crew no longer put in the old effort. The Hawks had that vibe of a sclerotic political entity, one that can only change on the day the aged ruler leaves office on a gurney. Wirtz had read enough good lit at Brown to avoid Lear's mistake. He kept the power. The king's men in the front office, lacking alternatives, obeyed whatever directives he passed down through the haze of illness or indifference.

That's my version, anyway. Others exist. I'd be the first to admit there's no reason to believe the inner workings of a hockey team parallel history or, for that matter, Shakespeare. There's also no reason not to believe it.

Skimming the early aughts also does a disservice to memory, to our shared past as fans. These Blackhawks teams created the worst era for the franchise since the 1950s, when shenanigans in team ownership led the Hawks to languish as a colony of the Red Wings. True, in the 2000s other teams didn't give the Hawks players to keep them in business. Unfortunately. Nor did the rest of the league treat them like a chain gang, as when the Wings sentenced star and team captain Ted Lindsay to Chicago for trying to organize a union. The 2003–04 Hawks of Mark Bell and Tuomo Ruutu, though wretched, at least were composed of men enjoying the full benefits of union-led emancipation.

When I went to games in those days it was always on impulse and always alone. It seemed unfair to ask friends to put down thirty or forty dollars to witness a death march. To be honest, it embarrassed me to feel the need to prove I was loyal enough to watch the team at rock bottom. I knew it was a case of overcompensation because at home I watched them only on TV when I needed background noise for laundry or insomnia.

On a typical night the U.C. was so empty I could've had full sections to myself, sections I had never seen even part empty before. Scattered knots of believers bothered yelling during the National Anthem. Forget angst or excitement during the game. I felt buyer's remorse.

Hawks management owed us all a refund just for reducing the crowd, always one of the best things about the experience, to a stupefied mass. More than once I even considered leaving at second intermission. Only a determination to witness the franchise's historic badness for future generations convinced me to go the distance. I had sat in the Wrigley bleachers the last day of the 1994 season, in spitting rain, watching players jog as if a paternity test waited at first base, and some part of me wanted to see if a game played by these Hawks ranked with that dispiriting experience.

It was worse, of course. That some of the Hawks tried hard made the whole experience of attending in person too sad for words. Blackhawks management had done the impossible. They had made pro sports look like a dead-end job.

At one game—in February, against the Sharks, during the only part of the season the Hawks weren't trudging through a giant losing streak—the only people near me were a family enjoying the food and a couple into each other far more than the game. Poor Alexei Zhamnov, eight years into his term as Purgatory's best player, either was about to get traded or had just gone to Philadelphia, a deal that left Bob Pulford with nothing to do but beg for years of patience.

Left to my drink and hot dogs, and with next to nothing at stake, I lapsed into inventing narratives to pass the time. After working through a lengthy story that involved Tyler Arnason and jumper cables, I gave Tuomo Ruutu a philosophical nature—I have no idea if the real Ruutu has one, though it's common enough among Finns—and had him deliver a soliloquy on how difficult it was to play out the string on a fifty-nine-point team. Then I remembered something. Back at my newspaper job in school I once wondered aloud about how hard it must be to play for the Cleveland Indians in September. At the time Cleveland had sucked since the 1950s. Dan, one of the editors, said it didn't sound so bad, in a tone that said volumes about the relative pleasures of playing pro baseball, regardless of record, to editing copy about junior college cross-country. We all laughed. The Imaginary Ruutu then adopted a shrug-and-bear-it attitude and looked forward to a nice meal once he got back to Helsinki.

I also thought up internal dialogues for the tough guys—Travis Moen and especially the popular Ryan VandenBussche. It must've been a difficult task to lace 'em up for punch-and-crunch duty given the state of the franchise. I know, they did it for their teammates. Even then, the call to duty must've been hard, you're taking punches to the face and ear, risking cuts and concussions, and for what? I'd have gone full on poignant had I known the Hawks would soon waive Moen and that the Bussche would be out of the league after the 2006 season.

I said a number of goodbyes in those days. To being single. To artistic pretentions. To the belief my country had a majority-sane population. A series of goodbyes, then, to parts of myself that had accompanied me on the bumpy trip to my mid-thirties. The cliché about letting go of youthful things kept coming to mind. Few things dated back longer in my life than the Chicago Black- hawks. The lockout, a certainty even as the 2003–04 campaign wrapped up, seemed the perfect time to make the break. I could blame all the owners, not just Bill Wirtz. It was like investing. You want to spread the negative feelings around.

Saying goodbye to being single involved a choice I made. After all, free will led me toward having my relationship with a woman consecrated before friends, family, the State of Illinois, and the desert god of the Hebrews.

Letting go of the Blackhawks presented thornier problems. I wanted to watch hockey. Replacing the Hawks was out of the question, however. I wasn't going to spend decades building up knowledge and memories around the Coyotes. Getting in the ground(ish) floor of the Wild held no appeal. I saw the Wings and Blues and Predators enough to know them and their history to some degree, but I hated Detroit and St. Louis and dismissed Nashville as minor league. As for a team from the East, the whole conference seemed foreign.

I moved in with my fiancé six weeks before the wedding. The new digs came with cable. How did the Blackhawks respond to this opportunity to play for my faltering love? By going 2-13-2 from March 3 on, with one of the wins against the sad-sack Capi- tals. It was a historic run, in a way. Even bad Hawks teams rarely challenged the 1938–39 team's 1-10-1 collapse.

That most of the losses took place at home spared me the ability to check in and see Minnesota take eight goals off the Hawks in front of half-filled U.C. I only recall watching parts of two contests. A tie with Colorado that somehow convinced me the bad times were over. (The Hawks then lost the rest of their games. Combined score: 30-12.) And on April 3, the night before my wedding, I watched a chunk of an overtime loss to Phoenix to distract myself from jitters. It worked. The Guinness helped, too.

The next afternoon I was at my wedding reception in an over-stimulated daze that made me wonder why I couldn't feel my legs. The Stars, meanwhile, beat the Hawks to tune up for the playoffs. My main interest in the box score was curiosity over whether Hawks goalie Jocelyn Thibault knew enough about the Civil War to pay a substitute to take his place. Apparently not. He let in five goals, including two by the brutish Shayne Corson—a third of Corson's season total. Maybe Jocelyn couldn't feel his legs, either.

TRYING

25

We honeymooned in Montreal. The Habs were in the playoffs. Tempted to watch in a bar with crazed Francophones, in the end I saw very little hockey, as the city and my wife provided excellent entertainment.

Not that I totally failed in my duty. Once we'd dumped the luggage at the hotel we walked the six or so blocks to the Bell Centre. I put my hands on the walls, had my wife take a picture I've since lost, and admired the gigantic player pictures. I suppose Saku Koivu was up there and maybe hard luck Jose Theodore, then less than two years from failing a drug test because of his hair loss medication.

A march to the original Forum site was part of another day's plans. But we ran out of time. Crisscrossing Mont Royal lasted into the afternoon. Then St.-Viateur Bagel and a second bagel place took a while. Montreal-style bagels were a revelation, and I had to see how the guys baked them. We also studied the local Jewish guys with the giant fur hats—having married a foxy Jewess, I felt I had to get up to date on the astonishing range of Judaic dressing habits—and unbelievably ate in yet another restaurant.

We also went to a grocery store to feed my addiction to May West cakes. May Wests are what you eat if Little Debbies aren't killing you fast enough. To this day, I look up a Canadian foods website to almost order six boxes of May Wests. Fortunately, I don't understand milligrams, so I can never figure out if the price is a good deal or not.

Hockey did dominate my honeymoon shopping, however. In Quebec (City) I bought a sheet of commemorative stamps featuring Howe, Gretzky, and others. I can't find half my honeymoon pictures, but the stamps are in a frame.

I wanted to buy an archetypical Canadian book on hockey, too. Just to tell visitors, I bought this in Montreal.

A trip to a shop showed me something I'd never see at home: multiple shelves of hockey books. None of the hockey-related literature interested me that much. I mean, it doesn't take much to draw me in. I even thumbed a five-hundred-page biography of classic rocker Randy Bachmann, albeit in disbelief that the book existed. Besides a few books I already owned, the selection was a bunch of uninviting titles somewhat but not exactly like *Guy Lafleur Cooks . . . with Pheasant.*

We wandered into a store that sold hockey junk, including little die-cast Zambonis. Team-themed, collect them all, that sort of thing. The store had the Zambonis on huge discount. Shoppers had cleared most of the stock until two teams remained: the Blackhawks and the equally dire Canucks. Chicago's hockey team had sunk so low in the eyes of Montreal's tourists that the store could not give away a collectible with the Blackhawks logo. It was like the store crowdsourced the entire hockey world's contempt.

I bought the Canucks toy. I had paid the Hawks enough money, merci beaucoup. I felt bad, anyway. What if a Hawks player back home for the summer walked into the store? It had to hurt to see that you skated with the likes of Vancouver, maybe even Atlanta, in the gutter of collectible irrelevance.

I considered one side trip: InGlasCo (Industrial Glass Company) headquarters in Sherbrooke, a city east of Montreal. InGlasCo makes pucks for the National Hockey League, three thousand of them for each team, each year. But I had known my new spouse a long time. A solid foundation of marriage rested on me not asking her to tour a puck factory when she could be ordering French cuisine. Following the Hawks had left me too dispirited to drive halfway to Maine, anyway. My God, on my wedding day they had wrapped up a season where they finished five wins behind the Blue Jackets and won twice in their last twenty games. Their leading scorer: strip-club patron Tyler Arnason, who played like a surly Gallic retail clerk. He'd get you an assist, if there was one on the shelf, but he wouldn't hurry, or like it, and go check in the back are you kidding?

The Hawks missing the playoffs saved me from having divided attention on my honeymoon, from, in fact, turning the honeymoon into the reason for my divorce. Tampa marched to an unexpected title that, to this day, no one takes seriously. The NHL was officially ridiculous, no better than baseball, with its revolving-door rosters cheered on by ahistorical fans as mercenary as the owners and players.

Bettman made the lockout official on September 15. Not a moment too soon, as far as I was concerned.

HIGH ANXIETY

26

Braced by maturity, bludgeoned by five solid years of hopelessness, I could live with another human being without subjecting her to Blackhawks-related moods. Other kinds, though, remained a problem. I had started to consult a professional five years earlier, having grown tired of anxiety and romantic misadventure and an Arnason-level of indifference to my work. Though counseling helped—I could never have married without it—I had a crash course in life waiting for me after the honeymoon.

One of the disadvantages of marrying late is that it rushes you to catch up with the signifiers others have already reached, or at least saved for. Baby. House. Détente with the partner's neuroses and blind spots and childhood. Agreement, however uneasy, on what constitutes a luxury and a necessity. Trying to tackle that all at once was crazy, on both our parts. Since we know how things turn out for the Blackhawks, let's put aside any pretension to suspense and say all of the above and more besides led to the end of the marriage.

Therapy was not up to dealing with the situation. I had no more idea how to be a patient than I did a husband. Once a week I met with a woman who listened to me go on about my doubts, problems, and anger. She gave me an objective observer's advice. She laughed at my jokes.

I went into the process with what I considered a good attitude. While I felt I had none of the usual hang-ups about masculinity and seeking help, I recognized those very hang-ups kept me from making the most of the sessions. Like a lot of people I wondered why I needed to go. I could make friendships, had scored an attractive and desirable wife, lived in a condo on Lake Shore Drive, and slept in a warm bed. More often, I resented the need to go and—again, like many people—often pondered on what was wrong with me, and why, questions my therapist and wife could have answered by ticking off reasons, though they would have needed an abacus to keep count.

I learned a great deal about myself, nonetheless. Not enough to get over my lack of satisfaction, with myself in particular, but I did make decisions from a more informed place, and with greater clarity. That many of these life choices ended in disaster said nothing about therapy, and a great deal about how messed up I'd been in the first place.

In all these sessions, I doubt I ever mentioned the Blackhawks. Keep in mind, often I spent these valuable fifty-minute periods in a state of anxiety over immediate, short-term problems, rather than childhood and primal fears. Yet somehow hockey, forever on my mind, never rated as important enough to bring up to my therapist, not even when the buyer's remorse over a ticket bled into several days. I'd prioritized the Blackhawks right out of my top ten of worries. In a sense, I think, the Hawks served as a manageable neurosis. It sounded crazy, when I had accepted intellectually that my actions had no effect on their play, but the Hawks filled in for all the problems I couldn't face. When I looked at my past failures and current fears, it paralyzed me. But the Hawks—

they didn't *really* matter, except as an entrée to catharsis, a way of practicing the anger, grief, bafflement, frustration, and all the other emotions I never wanted to feel and never learned to express.

Given my DNA and lack of will power, I could have fallen into chemical or liquid dependency to cope. Yet I dodged real life in ways that seemed benign by comparison—writing, ice hockey, depression (okay, not so benign), and a few other obsessions. What life I had began to seem lame. Worse, it seemed at odds with both masculinity and nonconformity. "I don't even have the imagination to destroy myself in a romantic way," I said to my therapist and my wife.

Around this time I swung into the deepest trough I had ever experienced, one of those states of utter numbness that leads to robotic interactions with others and hours-long staredowns with nothing. This depression had nothing to do with the ongoing NHL work stoppage. I say that in humor, but given the themes of this book maybe it bears pointing out, just to keep the record straight.

One of the few pleasures I remember experiencing at the time, in fact, was following the league's lockout. For a little while each day, I fled to a high-brained intellectual sphere concerned with worker-employer relations in the twenty-first century. The usual propaganda flew from both sides. Yet it lacked the entertainment value of past NHL scandals. The boys came up with nothing like Chelios's threat against Commissioner Gary Bettman's family during the 1994–95 dispute. It was just an ordinary, rotten sports labor war—petty, frustrating, frequently stupid, almost always dishonest, and at last a demoralizing failure by the players to practice the teamwork and never-say-die attitude they repeatedly evoked in their postgame interviews.

Bill Wirtz did his best to inject a little hockey gossip here and there. "I have great enthusiasm for the future," he said before busting out his talent evaluator's shtick:

A guy could be very talented, but is he willing to pay the sacrifice in the big league? I was happy to see [Matt] Ellison the other night. Do I like him? Yes I do. We've had [Igor] Radulov up here and [Mikhail] Yakubov. You have to see them play up here.

If you don't remember any of these guys, it's okay, Bill was just blowing smoke anyway. The stoppage never seemed to bother Wirtz that much. Oh, he said it did, the man knew public relations, but the battle had been coming a long time, and, from an owner's point of view, it was necessary. Rocky Marciano himself had punched Wirtz into unconsciousness and a jail cell during Dollar Bill's college years. What did he have to fear from a union with a divided membership roiled by more than a few restless bumpkins?

The stoppage taught me an overdue lesson: hockey players chummed bullshit like any other interest group. I'll also own up to the fact my political leanings led me to think the players might hold out for a deal more in line with what we see in baseball or basketball. Instead, they deferred to ownership, as hockey players have throughout the league's history. Jesus, the Red Wings lowballed Gordie Howe for decades, saying behind their hand that he made the most money on the team. When Gordie realized that was bunk, and *finally* demanded something closer to his worth, Wings owner Bruce Norris told Mr. Hockey, "Gordie, you never asked for anything more. I'm a businessman." That was the history the union played down to.

The players just wanted to play, we heard. So they did, for less than their worth, and under a structure that strips down the best teams for parts every two or three years. Every time I watched guys skating past the sad THANK YOU, FANS signs painted on the rinks, I again marveled at the cynicism of it all, but felt a purer amazement when I realized the cheesy, cheap ploy would work. That brand of lowball appeal *always* worked in hockey. The sport maintained an inexplicable innocence, its ongoing denial of reality clinging to an image of the past that, like most nostalgia, is stultifying and false. The NFL veered into spectacle, gladiatorial combat by way of Vegas and Michael Bay. The NBA embraced hip-hop and high fashion and celebrity. The NHL's big brainstorm, by contrast, was to send players onto blizzardy outdoor rinks and have both Mike Emrick and the league's official sponsors conjure images of little boys shooting a puck between a couple of old buckets.

The NHL had ceased its attempts to mainstream the product. From then on, it played to a narrow community of die-hards already snared by the game. I suppose this had a punk side to it, like the league had turned its back on arena rock and returned to the sound we all loved on those early albums. But it was an admission of defeat.

PURE PLATINUM

27

The labor dispute finished, the Hawks replaced the Pulfordosaurus at general manager with former announcer and team exec Dale Tallon. Tallon had a long history with the team as a player, as Foley's longtime partner in the booth, and in a couple of executive positions. You would think anyone would be an improvement on Pulford, and you would be correct, but Tallon's promotion reeked of the in-house cronyism that had crippled the team for years.

Peter Wirtz, son of Bill, provided the requisite kiss of death. "We feel Dale can take us to that next era. It's a new beginning for us. He's going to bring a new vision for us."

It was hard to imagine a new vision from a guy employed by the Blackhawks since the 1970s. Peter Wirtz owned the food service part of the family empire, though, so maybe he was just flattered someone asked him a question.

Tallon fired the head coach, hired a new head coach he kept for barely a year, and set a goal of finding "character players"—oh, God, pull the other one—to fill the locker room. He did spend money, and ate a fair amount of it, and by 2006 faced the fate of all Blackhawks honchos: replacement by Bob Pulford.

The biggest problem remained. The team would never move forward as long as Bill Wirtz remained alive. Not willing to wish him dead (abducted, maybe; retired, for sure), I accepted fate, found pleasure trying to cheer the players into competence whenever they played the Wings and Stars, and watched the moves of upper management as a sometimes-amusing play written to illustrate the supremacy of folly in human affairs.

The Hawks seemed determined to plumb that theme, too. Here we had a team in a seven-year swoon and not all that far removed from seeing three of its name players involved in a fight at a strip club in Columbus, Ohio—

Okay, wait, we must examine Theo Fleury's strip club brawl, for it defined an age.

No judgment on the strip club. Pro athlete or car salesman, spend your free time any way you like. We must put the affair in context, too. Hockey players were and are young millionaires trained to let their testosterone flow while maybe not yet being fully possessed of mature judgment. Except the three Hawks involved allegedly included Theo Fleury (age 34) and Phil Housley (age 106), two more over-the-hill once-stars hired to move merchandise, plus (allegedly) the always-winning Tyler Arnason. One night in 2003, having flown to Columbus after a tilt against the Blues, three Hawks players attended the show at Pure Platinum, a strip club at the edge of town. Around 4:30 a.m., police arrived to find Fleury bleeding in a pool of vomit. Outside a strip club in Columbus freaking Ohio. Not New York. Not Las Vegas. Columbus. In the aftermath, the usual suspects commented on the scandal without ever mentioning that going to a strip club in Columbus was the most embarrassing part.

Fleury later admitted he spent his time in Chicago determined to kill himself via a hair-raising series of adventures he undertook in response to the sexual abuse he had suffered in his teens. Once he told his story, his decline—the failed drug tests, punching a mascot while playing for the Rangers—made sense. That the Hawks signed him for eight million dollars did not, of course.

Anyway, what in the moment qualified as a public relations catastrophe was not long in the past when the team blamed Pat Foley, of all people, for its problems. Citing "recent circumstances," so who knows, the Blackhawks put a toe-tag on Foley, next stop Palookaville. Hawks management cited personal reasons that, you had to figure, didn't involve a visit to a college-town titty bar.

It was dumb and more evidence that Hawks management refused to tolerate even the reserved and justified truth-telling that Foley let into his broadcasts from time to time. In fact, Foley should've started each game by telling us we were wasting our damn time and turn the channel already, *Iron Chef* is on and they're cooking with octopus. With Foley out, Wirtz and his factotums remained the only certainties in Hawk fandom, unless you counted joylessness.

ON INJURED RESERVE

28

The honeymoon period had just passed when my wife and I had to deal with the long illness and death of a parent, my depression, money problems (often caused by me), emergency surgery (me again), and a heated, debilitating difference of opinion on whether or not to buy a house at the height of the most infamous housing bubble in American history. That was in addition to the usual newlywed adjustments.

I look back at that list and can't believe we eked out six-plus years. Our time together was not horrible until, say, the fifth year, that is, it paralleled the arc of a long-term contract for a thirty-year-old goaltender, except we couldn't loan the marriage out to a team in Switzerland and call up a new one from the minor leagues.

For a long time I'd half-believed, in that part of my brain maintained as a hardened bunker by my twelve-year-old self, that I bore some level of responsibility for the Hawks' fortunes. I never worked out quite how much. It related to superstition, I guess, and made as little sense; but somewhere in there, the pre-adolescent told me that a flawlessly reasoned letter to the Blackhawks' home office would turn the team around, if I could just articulate The Truth I possessed.

Having to care about housing prices—to say nothing of facing possible death or disfigurement from septic shock—blasted down the walls of that twelve-year-old's domain. It took a while to drag him out through the blare of second-tier Queen albums, but the process, once begun, could have only one end: the realization that my presence did not matter. Next stop? Ordinary fandom.

● Two weeks before my surgery, Bill Wirtz died in the very same hospital. I thought about him quite a lot after the doctors reserved me a room there. Despite my long at-a-distance relationship with the man and his works, his passing failed to spark a reconsideration of his career. An oddly indifferent reaction, considering how much thought I'd expended on the man over the years. A fair amount of my identity as a hockey fan formed as a reaction to his persona, his decisions, and the mythology that sprang up around him, as it springs up around any well-known plutocrat in control of a beloved product. Being a sucker, I granted that he had his complexities, and that he inspired real affection, respect, and gratitude in the people in his orbit. Yet next to no one who knew him only as a public figure shared those emotions, especially by 2007. I didn't know a single fan who wished him dead or one who mourned him. His passing even failed to evoke nostalgia.

It soon became clear that we'd rightfully suspected him of trapping the Blackhawks in amber. Almost immediately the home games landed on television and successful executives joined the team and management finally made about four thousand other necessary decisions. Every long-form story on the Hawks' post-2010 golden age references his passing as the turning point. A sad epitaph, when you think about it, for the hands-down most important figure in team history.

I had one of those surgeries where hospital techs get you up on your feet the next morning to walk, even though you feel like you just finished your ten-thousandth sit-up because a doctor removed a great length of your large intestine. For days I accompanied an IV pole around the floor, too stoned to figure out my sister-in-law's iPod beyond playing "Dear Prudence."

In the silences, I found I had put aside my everyday stress about work and money. I realized how unhappy I felt with my life. Rather than getting down, though, I resolved to take on these problems once I got out of the hospital. I spent the walks sorting out what I needed to change and rehearsing how to approach my equally unhappy wife on what seemed, even in a state of drug-addled optimism, very difficult problems indeed.

That was daytime. Even with morphine and boredom, I had trouble breaking my night owl habits, and while I needed to sleep by 8 p.m., an inability to do so left me with the television. Somewhere in there I returned briefly and tried to watch Hawks-Stars on a Saturday night. But morphine made hockey incomprehensible. Instead I sat in the room's recliner, distracting myself from thoughts of food—by then I hadn't eaten in days—and by pondering solutions to my problems.

Life, unlike hockey, doesn't have seasons. This is one of life's real drawbacks. I could pretend to start over on New Year's, or my birthday, or with the coming of spring. But all the mishegas carried over and I couldn't trade it for someone else's mishegas to see if that mishegas fit in better. Nor did my recent problems net me a top draft choice—say a doctorate in a technical field—that did as much to change my life as Jonathan Toews and Patrick Kane did to change the Blackhawks. The more I thought, though, the more I considered that maybe I had just blown my picks. In the past few years I had used the draft to add a terrific woman, the nicest home I had ever lived in, and a New York literary agent to what should've been a pleasant life. That should have fortified me as much as the Toews-Kane perfecta protected the Hawks against drafting a bust in 2008.

I emerged from the hospital convinced I had acquired a little wisdom. Sure of the road ahead and confident my wife and I could find a way, I got healthy and, more importantly, carried through some of my life changes. My father-in-law's death shelved the relationship discussions for a while, but, overall, I felt stronger and more hopeful than I had in years.

None of it worked out, in the end. But at least the Blackhawks got better.

THEY'LL NEVER GET PAST DETROIT

29

Cliché can speak truth. For instance, a life-threatening illness does clarify your thinking. So much so I wonder if Dale Tallon had one in 2006, because at about the same time he began to make prescient trades and other moves that set up the Hawks for the heights they'd reach after his departure.

Long used to soap opera and deceit, I marveled that the Hawks, of all teams, surged on a wave of competence and professionalism. The new owners only piped up to be bland. Joel Quenneville seemed like the stereotype of an old-fashioned hockey coach: non-controversial, ulcer-ridden, workaholic, only occasionally red-faced with rage, and generous with postgame cigars. Jonathan Toews threw down postgame clichés like a fifteen-year veteran while Patrick Sharp and Duncan Keith came across as the well-spoken beefcake necessary in our visual era.

I had a lot of time to catch up, with the economy ruined and all. As no jobs existed outside of North Dakota, at least I could watch games free of guilt. (My wife and I had put in our vows that, come what may, we would never move to North Dakota. "No Jews," she said.) The economic situation may have oppressed me, as it did millions of others, yet I believed better times waited just around the corner. The Blackhawks revival buoyed up the raw material of a wounded but very real optimism. For the sake of narrative, and appearances, I'd have preferred to take inspiration from a newfound love of a fashionably obscure art form, say, Weimar-era cabaret. But I had to some degree accepted my own helplessness vis-à-vis hockey, just as I had realized no amount of anger on my part would restore the value of my house or cause a hundred financial executives to plunge into a river of acid.

Wisdom, my new friend, told me the Hawks remained a few years away. I let myself get worked up during games, but not too worked up. Rather than see 2008–09 as a campaign, I figured it for the first leg of a three-year journey to—well, whatever the Toews-Kane-Keith-Sharp core had as their destiny. When the new Hawks defied the curse of the circus trip and nearly ran the table in December of 2008, it didn't bother me when wags and local cynics alike chanted, "They'll never get past Detroit." No kidding. The Wings rostered two or three Hall of Fame classes. I just wanted an appearance in the postseason.

It was a Hawks team I had never seen before, winning more with speed and finesse and increasingly keeping the tough guys in the press box. They still hit. Dustin Byfuglien was the human eraser. It just didn't seem to be the whole point of showing up. By New Year's, the Hawks appeared to bear out my measured hopes. They could beat anyone except Detroit. The Wings ended the Hawks' December run at the end of the month. Then they let the Hawks have the first period of the outdoor game at Wrigley Field before doing what visitors had done to Wrigley's regular tenant for a hundred years. The Wings later rested their stars to help the Hawks sweep a home-and-home at season's end.

It took an encouraging amount of overtime for the Wings to finish off the Hawks in the conference finals. The conference finals! The series inspired much pacing and pulling of hair—yes,

I pull my hair during playoff hockey games. Anyway, taking the loaded Red Wings to overtime on an almost nightly basis, once with Cristobal Huet subbing in goal, made the four-games-to-one loss not just palpable, but revelatory. I faced the discomfiting but proven truth that the Blackhawks were on the way up, and just how did I plan to adjust?

I had no idea, actually. The Blackhawks had not asked for a significant investment from me since the previous century. Though I had given them a fair amount of my short time on earth anyway, I found it a daunting prospect indeed to commit to a winner the way a true fan had to commit when one's team entered the running for the Cup. I mean, entered for real, beyond delusion. The loss to Detroit seemed like an aggravating but necessary stepping-stone, particular as time itself would add another layer of barnacles to the Wings' aging roster. It was not in me to feel confident, of course, but if the Hawks were for real I didn't want to miss the show.

The 2009–10 Blackhawks added time to my marriage. First, they provided an ongoing distraction, often in the evenings, when my wife and I might have otherwise fought (or, God forbid, communicated). Second, they provided me with a much-needed emotional outlet, as real life battered me with feelings beyond coherent articulation. Third, the combination of those factors kept Elizabeth and me together long enough to conceive our daughter. Finally, the Hawks' success, particularly their lights-out early season, continued to provide much-needed injections of optimism. If the sorry Blackhawks could claw back from the brink, I thought, no cause is lost.

Hope released such a cascade of endorphins that the offseason struck me as light-hearted farce rather than another manifestation of the franchise's death instinct. Or maybe I was just kidding myself because I knew, deep down, they might trade Toews for Pit

Martin. The team did spice up the climb to the top by flirtations with self-destruction. Tallon tried to snow the salary-cap sentinels with an amusingly dishonest contract that drew out payments to Marián Hossa for years. Years later *Grantland* labeled it "one of the most egregious examples of the blatant [salary] cap circumvention deals." But a Hawks exec playing con man was the best part. Here was deviousness harnessed to pull off the kind of slick move reserved for the well-run marquee teams.

The summer ended with a bit of minor, if weird, negligence involving free-agent paperwork that cost the Hawks some cap room and Tallon his job.

Also, Patrick Kane and his cousin roughed up a cab driver.

Also, Hossa had a serious shoulder injury.

So, the new season began ominously, with Hossa on the shelf, a new GM in his first GM job, Kane able to get into bars legally, and the Blackhawks in Helsinki to play the Panthers. I had watched the Hawks undone countless times by the annual West Coast swing. What would Finland do to them?

They rocked the entire early season, coming back from five goal deficits and other nonsense and growing stronger each month. San Jose shaped up as their main competition. Finishing second to them was the de facto hot spot, because the Sharks weren't going to do anything with home ice advantage in the playoffs except choke it away. Even the President's Cup seemed possible.

As the Hawks ascended to the contender tier, and the stakes rose, my anxiety-fueled superstitions returned. If my eye itched during a game, I scratched it. Then I scratched the other eye. I would scratch each four times, or eight times, as if composing in one of a strange form of music native to highland New Guinea. Ditto rubbing my nose. One friend asked me if I'd become a cocaine addict. I also went back to not moving during tense moments. If leaning forward, say, I remained that way, sciatica be damned, until the whistle sounded, or the Hawks made a mockery of my posture voodoo by allowing a goal. At times I had to pace to let off pent-up anxiety. Bad stretches of play I passed in the kitchen, or by maniacally switching channels. The contortions made me ache, but not until the playoffs began.

One might reasonably say I should've spent that time trying to salvage my marriage and job prospects. I did attend to the latter. After all, I had time on my hands. When the whole of American business decided to consider only applicants who had worked within the last six months, I sent resumes, guided by Grezkyian logic that said if you shoot enough times, the puck will go in. One might also reasonably say using hockey to escape my problems a few times a week improved my chances of staying sane, *sane* being relative, obviously.

THE YELLOW BRICK ROAD

30

I lived in Wilmette, the affluent suburb where Babyface Nelson died and Bill Murray grew up. Wilmette is the kind of North Shore community that attracts people who can afford to put their sons in an expensive club sport requiring a significant outlay for gear and travel. New Trier, the public high school serving the area, runs out boys' and girls' hockey teams that annually contend for state titles. Kids of all ages drag around thyroidal equipment bags. It's a town where you don't have to drive long to see a sign with the phone number of a guy willing to build you a backyard rink, though many families put them up in the front.

The spring of 2010 in Wilmette inaugurated a rite new to me: a proliferation of Hawks jerseys, flags, hats, window decals, and vanity license plates. Boys missing a few milk teeth busted out their customized Patrick Kane sweaters— always Kane, the moms wore Duncan Keith— and more often than not in Wilmette you'd see Kane's autograph on it, thanks to Dad being a season-ticket holder. Faced with these enviable totems, I packed away my pathetic starter jersey and brought it out only during the playoffs, and then to hang it in the front window, with its unadorned polyester protected from close inspection by shrubs and a Japanese maple.

It was rare to stand at the center of a craze I

understood. Friends new to Blackhawks fandom quizzed me. Some ten-year-old, seeing me as the picture of al fresco chill in my Hawks stocking cap in early May, with the weather seventy degrees, asked me about my favorite player, and we ended up in a debate about Dustin Byfuglien. The kid disliked him, to say the least. I remained bemused, indulgent of youth, but man, he was vehement, insisting Byfuglien did not belong on the same line as Toews and Kane, or maybe on the ice at all. I tried to gently steer the child's "Byfuglien coasts in the regular season" and "Byfuglien commits dumb penalties" charges in a more constructive direction. Byfuglien was destroying the Canucks. What else did the kid want? But he didn't care, and I watched him scooter away, secure in his wrong-headedness.

Meanwhile, the sportswriters and the internet wags and the haircuts on the newscasts gave us a gratifying stream of Hawksfotainment. Posters ran in the newspapers. Reporters filed feature stories from bars. There was ongoing commentary on players' beards. Duncan Keith brought the much-loved perennial topic of hockey dentistry into the spotlight by losing seven teeth to a puck against the Sharks. There was even a player with an ailing parent—Troy Brouwer's dad had undergone serious surgery.

Old-timers groused about bandwagon jumpers, as they do. But the whole rigmarole—from suburbanites in their new jerseys to the Twitter account started in the name of Quenneville's mustache—felt validating. Now everyone loved the Blackhawks. I walked Wilmette's streets strutting like preacher after a lights-out revival meeting.

● That a hockey team existed in Nashville was an anathema. Beyond that, though, I disliked the Predators only because I knew at least one elite team loses in the first round every season, and had to fear the Preds would make the Blackhawks that team. The

Hawks lost the series opener, and seemed an uncertain bet until a game-five OT win swung things their way.

The top two seeds in the East provided that year's sacrifices to hubris while the Blackhawks moved on to play Vancouver. Talk about a narrative. A team whose emotions ranged from bitch to moan, the Canucks were easy to hate on short notice, as one must in the playoffs. The previous hard-fought series in the 2009 playoffs, meanwhile, served as a nice table setter. Vancouver's goaltender, Roberto Luongo, had a reputation for mercurial play and spectacular collapses, so we had that to anticipate, while Daniel and Henrik Sedin, the twin brothers who shared the role of star forward(s), offered the worthy adversaries you needed for great drama. Alain Vigneault, the Canucks coach, stirred the pot with comments about Byfuglien's "illegal" play. Plus, for whatever reason, the Canucks decided to play tough guy to the Hawks finesse, giving Chicago the Gandhian moral high ground for probably the first time in franchise history.

It was fun.

The Hawks lost the first game at home 5-1 and never showed up. Every fan with a keyboard chimed in the next day in tones both anxious ("Maybe this is what they are . . .") and hyperbolic ("Vancouver in five"), though, when it came to expressions of discontent, nothing surpassed the third-period boos. The Hawks offered more of the lackluster same in game two. Vancouver dominated the first period and led after two. Luongo looked great behind a solid defense. Hawks players, meanwhile, kept losing their sticks. It was ridiculous. I was ready to resume the morphine drip when the Hawks summoned that thunderbolt we have all since come to recognize. Six or seven frenetic minutes undid the Canucks' all-around better effort. Having harnessed the unfairness of life to their cause, the Hawks marched west.

From there the series progressed in that wholly satisfying way achieved by a well-told story foreshadowed with perfection. Luongo melted down for five goals in the clincher, and Sharp rang a sixth off the iron. Daniel Sedin, legendary for his stoicism (it's an unemotional game), finished the series with roughing penalties on his score sheet. Byfuglien, never called for his supposedly illegal play, not only used Luongo for furniture but won the race to out-physical the other team when he and the corner boards compacted Canucks defenseman Alexander Edler. Brouwer even scored a goal for his dad.

It supposedly led to the Biggest Challenge Yet, the matchup with the San Jose Sharks that would demand the Hawks party less, do everything more, and count themselves lucky to survive. The prophesized classic series never shaped up. The Sharks went into another of their nose dives and the Hawks never looked back. Midway through the series, the random conversations went beyond the players everyone knew to in-depth analyses of the ham-and-eggers assigned to stop the best Sharks players. You know you are cheering for a winner when casual fans know the roster twenty deep.

FINAL-LY

31

Sports fandom trains us to accept that whoever wins the final game gets to call itself the best team in the league or, Americans being Americans, the best team in the world. We accept it, but a considerable minority refuses to believe it. The 2010 Philadelphia Flyers were as good an explanation as any for that hardy strain of agnosticism. Up and down all year, the Flyers made the playoffs only by playing the Rangers to a 1-1 tie in the last game of the season, then eliminating them in the shootout. The East went up for grabs in the postseason and Philadelphia emerged from the scrum. A team in their position—guys playing over their heads, with a clutch of comebacks and miracles in hand—normally enters the Finals as the lovable underdog. Fortunately, everyone hates the Flyers no matter what they do.

The Hawks, then, had the sentimental vote. None of their other advantages seemed formidable enough to inspire total confidence. No one in their right mind considered them favorites, for example, as to be in your right mind is to recognize the inherent unpredictability of the NHL postseason. The Flyers had already made history by roaring back from three games down to beat Boston, one of the rarest of sporting feats.

I felt better about this edition of the Hawks because they themselves seemed so unfazed by events. In 2015, I started to freak out, when they went down to the Ducks I think, and saw an interview where Brent Seabrook brought me back to earth by basically saying, "Eh, we've been here before, so what?" Looking back, the Hawks had some of that even in 2010, when they hadn't done anything yet. I told friends the Blackhawks had a real chance to win and—going out on a limb here—that they would not, WOULD NOT, get swept.

Determined to mine everything I could out of the experience, I put my Hawks home jersey in the front window and taped up a "4" written in thick black marker next to it. Others around town rigged up giant Hawks-themed inflatables, but I had a town-house association to contend with, and they were already on us for screwing up their award-winning landscape design with the Japanese maple, installed not long before by my sister-in-law and her nanny. In idle moments I dreamt of 2010 as a personal watershed year: my wife pregnant with our daughter and the Hawks in the Finals. I had forgotten I said something very similar to myself in 1992.

The Hawks put the team's last Finals appearance to rest by winning the first game. On the scoreboard, anyway. On the ice they reverted to the frustrating spot-'em-one-game group we'd seen against Nashville and Vancouver. Antti Niemi seemed at turns lost or in a greased-pig contest and even had a shot knock off his helmet. The Flyers goalie, former and future Hawk Michael Leighton, looked equally freaked out. The defenses teamed up to allow eleven goals, the kind of wide-open scenario that favored the Hawks.

Of all the narratives NBC tried to build, Flyers defenseman Chris Pronger turned out to be the most enjoyable. Pronger was the biggest name in the Finals. He had survived an age-nineteen debut in Hartford, a troublemaking youth, Mike Keenan, and an on-ice cardiac arrest to win an MVP award. Known for a certain wistfulness regarding the rules—he retired with eight suspensions in his jacket, a significant number for a star—Pronger had bounced from coast to coast. The Flyers were the third team in a row he'd led to the Finals. His size, Hall of Fame chops, and dirty tricks made him a worthy heel for any group of opposing fans.

He took over the series narrative due to his stardom and play, and because he never seemed to leave the ice. By the time the series hit its stride in Philadelphia, the media made him the center of all things, but, before that happened, the Hawks did their part to stoke the drama by complaining about his cheap shots. The Flyers as a whole tried to get rough in game two by starting future Hawk pest Dan Carcillo, Moe Howard on skates, a "physical presence" who's bullying often led to slapstick. As usual, Carcillo tried to hit everything including the Zamboni. It didn't have much effect except that Byfuglien stirred like a groggy monster in the depths of the sea. Also as usual, Carcillo smashed into one of his teammates and committed bad penalties. A couple of writers tried to turn him into a menace, but the Hawks clearly regarded him as a terrier you shake off your leg. Pronger, the real thing, popped Byfuglien in the neck, beat on Toews, and jawed at everyone.

The game only seemed close because the Hawks circled the wagons in the third period. Home ice defended, the series switched to Philadelphia.

Friends predicted sweep. True, the Hawks had answered whatever Philly tried to do. True, their success on the road had put them in the Finals. But I had my eye on game four because you had to grant the Flyers a win in their building. Pronger and their many good forwards would get a lift from the crowd and the law of averages and whatever else makes hockey players happier at home. I didn't stress out much during the game, even as Pronger's mischief enraged others. The Hawks played the Flyers even, forcing the game to overtime before the home team put a deflected shot through Niemi. Chicago's players seemed to have shaken off the loss before the postgame interviews ended.

Not the fans and writers, though. Pronger's legend grew, stoked by the announcers' incessant talk about him. Fans damned the Hawks for letting him get away with "it," it being the game he had played for the last sixteen years, a game recognizable to us because Pronger spent some of those years in St. Louis during an unusually acrimonious era in Blues-Hawks relations.

Pronger peaked as The Story at the end of game four, a not-great effort by the Hawks where the defense never got in gear. I spent most of the game as contorted as a yogi, trying to focus a combination of energies that would make Niklas Hjalmarsson quit giving away the puck. I'm not saying it worked, but the Hawks, outplayed for two periods, made the game close enough to pull the goalie for a chance to tie. It didn't happen. The Flyers had defended home ice.

Pronger, declared invincible by TV and internet alike, indeed forced the Hawks to change. Quenneville scattered his top players all over the place, always taken as a sign of weakness by announcers until it works. By the end of game five, Byfuglien had pounded Pronger to exhaustion, and the Hawks had scored seven goals. Pronger was on the ice for six and watched the other from the penalty box. Public Enemy Number One skated off looking half-dead, either from the punishment or from having to play so much or because of the knee injury none of us knew he had.

Seeing him vanquished was all anyone could talk about other than their plans for watching the next game. Even the gray-flannel *Tribune* put on clown shoes to run the infamous "Chrissy Pronger" image of the Flyers star in a dress. The *Tribune*. The nasal voice of bloodless Midwestern conservatism. A publication that delivered all the thrill of cardboard negligee. For the Blackhawks, of all things, the *Tribune* removed the stick lodged up its ass. Had Pronger really worn Vera Wang in a game, it would have been less shocking. "Sophomoric, demeaning garbage," said Jim Rome, incensed about the sexism angle. Had the world gone mad?

Playing it cool, the Blackhawks said nothing about skirts or much of anything else beyond the boilerplate. Early on in game six, with Leighton down and out, Toews couldn't quite put his stick on a fluttering puck, but the Hawks got into their groove. Pronger went off late in the first, and Byfuglien, free of the only guy who could handle him, finished off one of those Hawks pinball passing displays from in front of the net. Niemi stopped a breakaway about forty seconds into the second, but a fast break and Duncan Keith falling down put Daniel Briere behind the D and gave the Flyers the lead.

It turned into a dead-even game where the last bounce or savvy move wins it. The Blackhawks would play many of those games in future years, would finish Boston and Los Angeles in just that way, and would lose to the Kings that way, too. But in 2010 I had yet to realize this version of the team had put the past I had lived far behind, that they shared a jersey with my heroes of yore but not a lot else.

The Hawks tied and went ahead. Frozen by fear, I went into OCD mode. For all the good it did. The Hawks fell back on their heels. To say the least they looked unsure, not worried or nervous, just unsure. Niemi lunged forward to stop a wide-open shot that, I am not ashamed to say, made me scream.

Philly almost won in the first few seconds of overtime—Niemi, again sprawling forward, smothered the puck—and anything could happen. Four minutes later, anything did. Kane worked a head fake and took an impossible shot.

The puck went into a black hole. No one has seen it since.

"I don't think anyone saw it in the net," Kane said later. "I booked it to the other end. I knew it was in. I tried to sell the celebration a bit."

"It's in, it's in," I screamed, for all the neighborhood to hear, but it was more hope than anything, until Kane flew down the other side of the ice, chased by his teammates, the building dead quiet, announcer Mike Emrick trying to make sense of the situation until the replay showed the puck jogging the inside of the net.

"It's in," I repeated, breathless. "I don't believe it. They won. I don't believe it."

BEFORE THE PARADE

32

The next day, after the breakfast conversation with my wife, I went out to burn off the substantial adrenalin that remained. Wilmette spreads out, and I walked a fair amount of it, taking parole for the morning from work and the other killjoys of adulthood. A major road, Lake Street, runs east to west, indexing the suburban sprawl. At one point a number of side streets jut off from it, leading to an area heavy with Native American street names: Seneca Road, Pontiac Road, Chippewa Lane, a bunch of others. A week or so later I read that a thief or thieves had stripped Blackhawk Road of five of its signs. That's love.

Of all the events I hoped to see as a child or adolescent, I had waited longest for two: the publication of a novel, and the Blackhawks winning the Stanley Cup. Both happened within a few years of one another and, on reflection, left me in similar states—overjoyed, of course, over the frigging moon, and exalted, as if I might ride the triumph to a new self, a new life made up equally of nurtured dreams and stunning surprises. But I also felt breathless and stunned, wondering what could come next. I am sad to say I most of all felt relieved, in a way I must crudely compare to losing one's virginity. I could analyze the emotion with clarity of mind because I had felt the same relief not long before, when my wife informed me that the pregnancy test in a box had come up a winner after trying for that result had taken six years and a big part of our marriage from us.

Bringing it around, then, I contemplated on what the players themselves might feel. They had summited their Everest. Whatever else happened, they had experienced a dream that came out of the deepest part of themselves, a dream that for some of them went back as far as memory itself. What must it be like to feel that sense of accomplishment? To trade in the yearning for the having in a fundamental part of your life?

What must it be like to have a tangible marker of success that elevates a person to the top of his chosen career? An Oscar, the Pulitzer—gaudy honors, sure, but to some degree the fruits of a popularity contest. What the Hawks had won required them to do more than their jobs. They had to accomplish the work while another group of opponents just as determined, just as pain-tolerant, just as consumed by the same dream, put forth an incredible effort—an insane effort, by any measure recognized by mainstream society—to stop them. I mean, I can rail at Fate for falling short of my dreams, but Fate never cross-checked me in the neck while trying to steal my computer.

I also wondered if, at the end, these guys experienced a moment of peace. Professionally speaking, for them there's nothing *beyond* a Stanley Cup. Winning it must free you, for a little while, anyway, from a pressure to perform that most of us cannot imagine. Think of it. A Stanley Cup game is by definition historic. If an athlete fails to perform on that hallowed ice, the circumstances turn him to stone and stand him in the museum of team history, his transgression a chapter in fan lore or, in the most egregious cases, part of the lore of the game itself. He must show up no matter how sick his father, how strained his home life, how painful his knee or teeth or hip, how uncertain the next contract. If you fail, the boos of fans and railings of journalists mean nothing next to facing teammates you've disappointed, and management paid to judge how you did your job in a milieu intolerant of excuses and unable—for the sake of its own survival—to forgive human failings. Then that night comes when you kiss the Cup, and for once no fan, no teammate, no coach, no media hustler can honestly ask more of you. You don't even have to ask any more of yourself, for a little while.

That train of thought says more about my place in the world on that June day that it says about the Blackhawks. No doubt the players, after all the hard work and pressure and physical punishment, appreciated what they had done. Then again, they were young men, a demographic filled with units famously incapable of perspective. Anyway, I was thrilled for them and for myself. On my walk I took note of every flag and grotesque inflatable, every jersey on every kid, and every newspaper box with a picture of the Stanley Cup celebration inside. Each manifestation of this community hysteria lifted me past mere relief, to happiness, for a little while.

PACIFIC DIVISION

33

A lot happened between 2010 and 2013. To condense, I watched the second run to the Cup in Los Angeles. I had spent every day for twenty-six months caring for my daughter and, now forced to live without her, all but lost my mind. But late in 2012, I knew my wife and I could not remain in close proximity, and, given a choice between two kinds of pain, I chose the one I could bear.

I experienced the Hawks' second postseason triumph with, as they say, an open heart. Walking around as a pulsing wound is a bad state of being that nonetheless opened me up to *all* my emotions. The 2013 Hawks elicited a joy—and terror, and amazement—I had no hope of feeling in 2010. I watched without cynicism, too, because the Hawks had already won the Cup, and if I wanted more, and I did, I no longer felt I could ask for it. Also mixed in there was a willingness, strange to me, to live the experience, to follow the Buddhist advice that suggests we remain always in the present.

The work stoppage that year played to the Hawks' strengths. A short season removed some of the need for depth, an area of uncertainty for the Hawks as they fought back from their post-2010 wrangles with the salary cap. Fewer games allowed teams to ride their elite players much harder, and the Hawks had elite players to match up with anyone. I was less surprised by the team's success than the fact my cockamamie preseason analysis predicted reality.

In Los Angeles I lived with sports-loving friends willing to join me in the revels, to egg me on to screaming along with the National Anthem, to tolerate my obnoxiousness. That was the evenings. By day I desperately tried to find work. I applied for everything from Target associate to writing for a leading Southern California life coach. When I could think of no more doors to knock on a particular day, I did my level best to walk out the pain, and to sweat it out and cry it out, to re-live all that I'd done, the thoughtless and the regrettable and the cruel. I starved twenty more pounds off my body. I shook and sweated from panic attacks. I resisted all the coping mechanisms that had fended off this necessary exorcism for the whole of my adult life. On my better days I enjoyed the city, even if my budget restricted me to long walks and iced tea and the La Brea Tar Pits, the last a good metaphor not only for my emotional state but for many human dilemmas. (Rousseau: Man is born free but everywhere he is trapped in tar.)

It was fun to watch the Blackhawks vie for the Finals with the Kings while on site. And thank God, because the first round with Minnesota delivered five games of slog-it-out attrition. The near miss versus the Red Wings, on the other hand, was just terrifying.

Detroit seemed to have figured out what announcers, argumentative ten-year-olds, and most others missed: that Jonathan Toews was the Blackhawks' engine. The Wings grabbed him, swatted him, clubbed him, mugged him, an all-front assault that had the Hawks sputtering and kept them to a single goal over games three and four. I knew I had matured a little because, though upset by the state of affairs, I could concede the Red Wings had figured out something important.

Down three games to one, the Hawks counterpunched. They

always seemed to own the middle section of a series, as if they had played rope-a-dope long enough to figure out the other team's approach and steadily pick it apart. Detroit looked flat in game five, and game six featured a thrilling Michael Frolik penalty shot that ended up being the game winner. Frolik was a case study in how the playoffs magnified subtleties. Known for a single skill—killing penalties—Frolik grew in stature as it became clearer the dead-even series might turn on one of those power plays Hawks fans counted on him to stop. Frolik's game-winner also served the narrative, if you liked that sort of thing. He set up the play by blocking a shot, flew after the puck and past the defense, and drew a smack across the hand that the referee, alone of just about anyone outside Chicago, thought deserved a penalty shot.

Detroit fans probably still complain about what happened, and not without reason, but the gods gave back Frolik's good fortune in game seven. A nerve-wracking 1-1 tie had gone into the late minutes. Frolik twisted into position and put a shot straight into Jimmy Howard, the Wings' goalie. Just under two minutes, and one of those moments took shape, when for once in hockey you could understand the game's calculus, Andrew Shaw along the boards with the puck, Bickell charging the net, not even looking for a pass, the entire center of the ice empty for what seems like minutes, before a red blur, Hjalmarsson, no one near him, skated in, it was like slow motion, Shaw sent the pass dead on, Hjalmarsson stick back, Hjalmarsson stick down, Howard the only guy in the way, the black dot of the puck banging off the far corner of the net—

"And they are waving it off."

I think I rewatch that play more than any other, and it never fails to thrill. The refs ignored beauty, as Authority often does, and did in fact disallow the goal. Sitting there in the moment, I imagined the years of complaining ahead for me and for all of us, and with Red Wings perfidy on top of it all, a cheap shot of Brandon Saad into the bench that caused an official to blow his whistle and saved Detroit. Wanting to seem a good sport for my friends, one of them a Wings fan, I shook my head and sighed. Ah, the whims of fate. Inside, I put philosophy on call to get me through the evening and all the future summers when the Hawks failed to make the Finals as they should have in 2013.

The winning goal—Seabrook in overtime—saved me from musing on the big questions, any more than I already did that.

The Kings series baffled me. Not the result. That I liked. But I never quite understood what L.A. wanted to do. Detroit had provided a template. Yet the Kings—a far more talented team than that year's Wings group and very much the Hawks' superior in brute strength—failed to key on Toews beyond the usual. Beyond that, they had a much-discussed inability to score on the road, and their Toews—Anze Kopitar—looked hurt. True, they took away space as advertised, bodying up guys after the puck, chipping away passes, sweeping everybody and everything to the margins. But the Hawks more or less coped.

Having figured on a seven-game series, I too was surprised to find the Hawks heading to L.A. with a two-game lead. A close game one had turned into an all-Chicago sequel that added to the Kings' growing list of casualties and forced Daryl Sutter, former Hawks captain and coach, to pull goalie Jonathan Quick.

The Hawks only needed a split in L.A. I felt sure they would lose game three. It's an NHL tradition for a desperate team to return home and win, and the Kings had the top home record in the league.

True enough, L.A. won, to such a degree that Kane, then in one of his sleepy stretches, came in for slams or, in Quenneville's case, a measured request that he do more. Like all Hawks fans, I expected Kane to save every game and in my frustration started calling him "Anakin" because he reminded me of actor Hayden Christiansen.

The seven-game prediction looked more likely as the league punishment office, awakening from its usual postseason torpor, suspended Duncan Keith for swatting L.A.'s Jeff Carter in the face with his stick. Anakin, though, came to life. Once paired with Toews again—Quenneville's nuclear option—Kane did what he does when he's on. The Hawks faced a chance to close it out in five games. Considering the Kings' desperation and Keith's absence, the development was nothing less than shocking.

In the clincher, Keith scored the first goal—pure Hollywood—and Kane scored three more. The Kings managed to tie the game twice, the second time with just a few seconds remaining in the third period, but all three Kane goals came with him wide open, and while I know stopping that sort of thing isn't easy with a guy like him, if I'd been an L.A. fan I would've been screaming, "How can he EVER be wide open?"

Even if the game took two overtimes, the Hawks had the best of it—Hossa two breakaways, Johnny Oduya on the doorstep, Brandon Saad setting off a goalmouth scramble, Kane with a pass to himself through a defenseman's legs before an awesome hip check sent him flying. He and Toews teamed for the winner—again Kane loose and at full speed, Toews running a parallel line, again one of those goals you could see shaping up to such a degree you could scream in advance.

● Is it a cop out to have next to nothing to say about the Bruins series? As far as my reactions to the play, the rest of this book—my narrative—provides the details.

I don't think hockey added to the panic attack I had at a library the day after game two, although had it been a heart attack, as

I feared, I would've entered the afterlife good and pissed that I checked out with the Blackhawks in the Finals. I conjured instinctual but no deep dislike of the Bruins from the air, fidgeted with the usual superstitions, and watched in awe as the Hawks once again put me through a shaky start to the series, and readjusted, and won. About the only thing I had learned since 2010 was how not to waste time. Sure of the result in game three at Boston, I refused to watch.

When Dave Bolland ended it in that impossible game six—two Hawks goals in seventeen seconds, Bolland's on a freak bounce off the post—an era of my life came to a happy end, soaked with sweat and on the floor hugging a Labrador. My reservoir of emotion for the Hawks at last ran dry. I could enjoy them, and cheer them on, but I have yet to feel that invested again, even in 2015, and I doubt it will happen. A few days after the Hawks finished the Bruins, as I mulled flight plans for Chicago, my wife asked for a divorce, in a voice so straightforward that it made me realize reconciliation was never on her agenda. With my hosts stating, understandably, that I'd reached the limits of my welcome, I flew home. A lot of suffering awaited me, but, unlike with the Blackhawks of old, none of it came as a surprise.

LADY BYNG

34

I can say without hesitation that cheering for a winner beats cheering for the underachievers, the hopeless, and the volatile. It will end, of course. A golden age always ends, and the salary cap now cuts into the precious half-life enjoyed by a great NHL team. One day, the core talent will get old or move on. No longer will the Hawks luck into a free-agent Russian who, hey presto, becomes Rookie of the Year. Other teams will land the Andrew Ladds of the trade deadline or the Jonathan Toews of the draft. The bounces will go the other way. Even the dumb little pleasures of belonging to this ongoing community experience will fade. No more Niklas Hjalmarsson modeling fashions in glossy local magazines. No more cheap T-shirts with players' names on the back at the grocery store checkout line. Even Pat Foley has to retire someday. The Blackhawks' seasons, shorter in truth, will become much longer in the watching.

When the team at last regresses to the mean— I'm not using the word in a mathematical sense— I won't miss the hockey-related agonizing they helped me exorcise. Nor, I believe, will I go back to it. What more can I ask of the Chicago Blackhawks? Oh, sure, in 2015, I hoped they'd beat Tampa Bay. I hoped for it acutely. I also knew I'd shrug off defeat if it happened. The Hawks had won two Stanley Cups. (Then they'd win a third.) Wanting more just invited a thunderbolt.

Though I think of four Cups, the equal of the Gretzky Oilers, and—

Okay, contradictions remain.

When it comes to hockey violence I suppose I have to live with my hypocrisy or find a new game. Like many fans I'm aghast over concussions and the epidemic of chronic traumatic encephalopathy brewing in the brains of God knows how many former players. Just look at the very narrow subset of players referenced in this book. We all know about Bob Probert. Mike Peluso came out in 2015 as suffering from seizures and depression and the sobering expectation he would die young. Jeremy Roenick, by his own admission, stumbles over words and suffers from memory problems. A months-long recovery from a concussion landed Stu Grimson in retirement. Then there's Steve Montador, not mentioned but a Blackhawk in 2011–12. Steve Ludzik, now struggling with Parkinson's disease. Dave Christian. Bernie Nicholls.

I cheered on all these guys. The Blackhawks marketed their style of play—a style that damaged all of them—to get money out of me, money I gave over without hesitation and certainly without any reflection on the mortality of the players. Even if no one knew about the dangers of concussions then—plausibly true of the players, less plausibly so when it comes to doctors—and even if all of them deserve their own agency and choices, I feel accountable, not personally, you understand, but as part of a culture that may send a substantial number of former players into self-harm, a greatly reduced quality of life, or the long dark of dementia. The league, to its credit, created a protocol for dealing with concussions, and though it comes in for criticism it exists, and can be refined. Alas, the league also employs a commissioner determined to sandbag on compensation for the generations of players treated like meat by the thirty client franchises who keep him in nice suits and the public eye. Who with the smoothness of a tobacco magnate drones on about how the science is not in. Who hires the lawyers who dispute the neurological problems of ex-players.

I suppose I also have to accept the presence of men like Bettman overseeing the sport, and the tiresome Wirtzes running the corner of it I love most. Mellowed by age, I react to Chicago hockey's first family with amusement as much as anger, though not without anger, you understand. For instance, Rocky Wirtz claimed the Hawks had yet to show a profit after three championships. Yes, yes, Rocky Wirtz changed the team culture, hired competent people, brought the organization into the new century, and made peace with the fractious team history orchestrated by his father. All credit due. But crying poor from atop one of the NHL's most successful franchises marks him as out of touch as others of his breed and tax bracket. On a good day, you laugh at this ridiculousness in self-defense (because you know it expresses Wirtz's contempt for your intelligence) and out of a sense of superiority (because you may not own a pair of $1,000 shoes, but you also have enough class to keep your delusions out of the public record). What if the Hawks really haven't shown a profit? If, to use a hypothetical example, all the money went to service debt accrued in the dismal aughts? You can still take comfort in the fact you don't expect strangers to worship you because you make the ultimate sacrifice of running at a loss the NHL team you owned a piece of on the day you were born.

Finally, I suppose I have to accept the changes in the game. I say this as someone who agonized over the elimination of the red line. I acquiesced to realignment and the renaming of the divisions as part of my nineties hockey evangelism, and of course to the rules changes that sped up the game and exploded the trap-heavy defenses of yore. All I can say of instant replay is that it's a necessary evil. The shootout will always be an anathema, but maybe the new three-on-three overtime will cause it to wither away. Old-timers, often cranky ex-players around my own age, complain now about the modern player's penchant for drama. I, too, could do without the diving and clutching at nicked faces and flamboyant falls. At the same time, players quell these habits during the postseason, as they do all the bad hockey habits, and, as the postseason makes up an increasing percentage of my hockey consumption, I see everyone at his best behavior. Also, I am uninclined to believe theatrical shenanigans never happened before 2008.

The higher-brain stuff—the game's economics and culture, the medical controversies and labor contretemps—keep me reading. But the game of hockey keeps me watching. Show me a Blackhawks game in progress and all the intellectual stuff vanishes under a tsunami of adrenalin. I used to think this marked me as a rube. A significant percentage of the women I've known agree with the assessment. They consider sports fandom more or less a character failing, not a serious failing, like spending too much money at Pure Platinum, but a yellow flag along the lines of wearing a beret. Having heard the criticism so often, I've reached for justifications of dubious provenance ("Hockey is unscripted reality TV") and, my old failing, unbaked intellectualism ("Hockey is no different than Mamet, except you don't know how a game will end").

I don't care much about the criticism anymore, though. I own my obsession, as the Los Angeles life coaches say, and even kid myself it's better than the obsession owning me. The passion remains. I just have more things drawing from the well, proof that, the opinions of women notwithstanding, I don't follow sports to fill in the holes of a sad, empty, regressed existence. I write books to do that.

Parenthood is the foremost of those competing passions right now. Raising a child offers a mystery that runs parallel with one of its joys. That joy is seeing your offspring change, grow, *become.* The mystery is how some of what he or she becomes was present at the beginning.

My daughter entered the world a mellow pacifist. She landed with a mother who nurtured her compassionate, easy-going nature, a woman who agreed that you should play *Chutes 'n Ladders* without a winner or loser. Lacking competitiveness, to say nothing of aggression, my daughter will not become one of the many American girls who strap on hockey pads nowadays. I cannot imagine her even approving of hockey, unless the league brings back ties.

Her mother takes her ice skating sometimes. The two of them stutter-step in that beginner's way around the boards of the park district rink while I watch. Sitting there I wish I'd had parents who encouraged me to ice skate, like the boys I'll see a few minutes later in the lobby, lacing them up for practice. On wistful days I think: It's not too late. I mean, you always read about some ninety-year-old in New Brunswick who's still playing in a local league.

When the free skate ends my daughter climbs into the bleachers next to me to watch the Zamboni. She's mad for Zambonis. I gave her the Canucks toy I bought on my honeymoon. It once played an important part in her playtime narratives, stories where Lego people and stuffed blue rabbits get into trouble involving toilets.

I was not much older than my daughter is now when hockey,

via mysterious paths, entered my psyche. What obsessions have already taken hold of her?

As the Zamboni rolled by us, we talked about the machine and the way it makes ice. I thought of how, over all those years, I could always go back to the Blackhawks. They gave me a haven and a practice field for my feelings, a distraction from my trials, and an entrée to community.

Maybe there on the bleachers I truly reach the end of my narrative with the team, the current narrative, I mean, the one started so long ago, and I kiss the top of my daughter's head, and realize that I've found another place to come home to, season after season.

SOURCES

p. 8: "This is the Oscar of hockey." Mikita, Stan. *I Play to Win: My Own Story*. New York: William Morrow, 1969.

p. 9: "Richard and I always . . ." Mikita, Stan. *I Play to Win: My Own Story*. New York: William Morrow, 1969.

p. 10: "We both wound up . . ." Mikita, Stan. *I Play to Win: My Own Story*. New York: William Morrow, 1969.

p. 20: "Glad I didn't have to do color . . ." Verdi, Bob. "Hawks defeat Seals, within 3 of lead: Pappin and Marks tally in 3-1 victory." *Chicago Tribune*. January 20, 1975, p. C1.

p. 20: "Chicago just puts you to sleep." Verdi, Bob. "Hawks defeat Seals, within 3 of lead: Pappin and Marks tally in 3-1 victory." *Chicago Tribune*. January 20, 1975, p. C1.

p. 23: "milieu control." Lifton, Robert Jay. *Thought Control and the Psychology of Totalism: A Study of "Brainwashing" in China*. Chapel Hill, NC: University of North Carolina Press, 1989.

p. 27: "We have gambled . . ." Reed, J. D. "Bye-bye Boston, Chicago buys." *Sports Illustrated*. June 21, 1976.

p. 28: "Last year our power play . . ." Gammons, Peter. "Return of the Fabulous Invalid." *Sports Illustrated*. October 18, 1976.

p. 30: "A cracked cheek bone . . ." Duhatschek, Eric. "Life was good for Magnuson." *Globe and Mail*. December 17, 2003.

pp. 30–31: "The young hockey star . . ." Unknown. *Toronto Star*. February 23, 1974.

p. 32: "I guess I was more . . ." Personal email. March 3, 2012.

p. 45: "Radio football is football reduced . . ." Hornby, Nick. *Fever Pitch: A Fan's Life*. New York: Penguin, 1992.

p. 48: "The Ministry of Natural Resources . . ." Matsumoto, Rick. "Secord off to a flying start." *Toronto Sunday Star*. October 18, 1987.

p. 48: "It was the left hand . . ." Unknown. *Toronto Sun*. April 21, 1987.

p. 48: "Secord's right leg . . ." Matsumoto, Rick. "Secord off to a flying start." *Toronto Sunday Star*. October 18, 1987.

p. 53: "Where hockey was concerned . . ." Goyens, Chrys. *Blades on Ice: A Century of Professional Hockey*. Markham, ON: TPE Publishing, 2000.

p. 57: ". . . plain-looking pudgy man . . ." Falla, Jack. "No squawks from the Hawks." *Sports Illustrated*. November 15, 1982.

p. 63: "The problem was that our guys . . ." Milbert, Neil. "Manson suspended for 13 games." *Chicago Tribune*. December 27, 1989.

p. 64: "He does not get paid . . ." Verdi, Bob. "Tough guy, tough game." *Tribune Sunday Magazine*. March 24, 1991.

p. 65: "When Dave Manson lost control . . ." Roenick, Jeremy, with Kevin Allen. *J. R.: My Life as the Most Outspoken, Fearless, and Hard-Hitting Man in Hockey*. Chicago: Triumph Books, 2012, p. 52.

p. 68: "Initially, Manson took his medicine . . ." Roenick, Jeremy, with Kevin Allen. *J. R.: My Life as the Most Outspoken, Fearless, and Hard-Hitting Man in Hockey*. Chicago: Triumph Books, 2012, pp. 52–53.

p. 75: "Chicago was a team bewildered . . ." Kiley, Mike. "Flames finish off Hawks." *Chicago Tribune*. May 11, 1989.

p. 77: "Dec. 1 Peter Worrell (FLA) . . ." Beaver, Mike. "Mixin' it up." *Village Voice*. January 26, 1999. Archived at: http://www.hockey-fights.com/forum/showpost.php?post/415990/

p. 77: "Dec. 5 Jeff Odgers (COL) . . ." Beaver, Mike. "Mixin' it up." *Village Voice*. January 26, 1999. Archived at: http://www.hockey-fights.com/forum/showpost.php?post/415990/

p. 85: "Soccer is popular . . ." Quoted in Mathew, Shaj. "Why did Borges hate soccer?" *New Republic*. June 20, 2014.

p. 87: "popgun offense." Kiley, Mike. "Hawks' popgun offense fails again." *Chicago Tribune*. December 27, 1991.

p. 91: "... to wear [the Penguins] out ..." Kiley, Mike. "Hawks flunk out again: Penguins take 2-0 lead." *Chicago Tribune.* May 29, 1992.

p. 91: "He has his reasons ..." Kiley, Mike. "Hawks flunk out again: Penguins take 2-0 lead." *Chicago Tribune.* May 29, 1992.

p. 94: "ubiquitous." Kiley, Mike. "Keenan gone, Hawks turn to Pulford again." *Chicago Tribune.* November 8, 1992.

p. 107: "He's going to be with us ..." Kiley, Mike. "Roenick a Hawk for life?" *Chicago Tribune.* February 13, 1994.

p. 109: "There are not many centers ..." Johnson, K. C. "Blackhawks trade Roenick to Phoenix." *Chicago Tribune.* August 16, 1996.

p. 112: "It seems like all you gentlemen ..." Strom, Rich. "Wirtz drops gloves, comes out swinging for Team USA." *Chicago Tribune.* March 13, 1998.

p. 121: "The loss dropped ..." Merkin, Scott. "Hawks down under, hit 42-year low at 20 below .500." *Chicago Tribune.* March 1, 1999.

p. 137: "I have great enthusiasm ..." Foltman, Bob. "Woe is Wirtz? Not a chance." *Chicago Tribune.* February 8, 2004.

p. 137: "Gordie, you never asked for anything ..." MacSkimming, Roy. *Gordie: A Hockey Legend.* Toronto: Greystone Books, 2003.

p. 139: "We feel Dale ..." Morrissey, Rick. "Wirtz's first move shows promise of change." *Chicago Tribune.* October 12, 2007.

p. 149: "... one of the most egregious ..." McIndoe, Sean. "Hockey's worst contracts." *Grantland.* February 13, 2014. Archived at: http://grantland.com/features/hockeys-worst-contracts/

p. 159: "Sophomoric, demeaning garbage ..." *Rome Is Burning.* Broadcast date: June 9, 2010. Archived at: https://www.youtube.com/watch?v=-zVMJxxpRg8

p. 160: "I don't think anyone ..." Klein, Jeff Z. "Blackhawks win first Stanley Cup in 49 years." *New York Times.* June 9, 2010.